SAVE YOUR MARRIAGE ALONE

A Step-By-Step Guide to Getting Your Spouse's Love Back in 90 Days

---

ANDRE SANTOS

Copyright © 2024 by Awesome U Coaching Inc.

All rights reserved. No parts of this publication may be reproduced or transmitted in any form without written permission from the author.

Additional Notice and Disclaimers

No guarantees, promises, or suggestions of any results are made, whether implied or stated. Individual results may vary from those shown, and everything herein is provided on an "at your own risk" basis.

Contents

Here's How To Work With Me To Implement This System That Saves Your Marriage In 90 Days	5
Introduction	7
Becoming a Relationship Jedi	13
Rethinking How To Save A Struggling Marriage	17
The Science of Connection	23
Step 1 - Decoding Your Spouse's Matrix	31
Step 2 - Go through a fast Neural Makeover	43
Step 3 - Dig them out of their Entrenchment	51
Step 4 - Pluck Thorns	59
Step 5 - Get them to chase you	67
Step 6 - Make them fall in love with you again	75
Step 7 - Correct their behavior with Psychological Qualification	83
Success stories	91
What To Do Next	105
About the Author	113

Here's How To Work With Me To Implement This System That Saves Your Marriage In 90 Days

Hey reader.

Andre Santos here.

I have one goal with this book: To give you the information you need to save your marriage without your spouse needing to be on board.

My best strategies, insights, and breakthroughs from using this system to save hundreds of marriages are in this book.

And even though that's the case, I still get quite a few people asking how they can get more personal help with implementing this.

So if you want us to hold your hand through transforming your marriage…

All you have to do is:

Go to *www.science-of-connection.com* to book a call with us.

Tell us a bit about your marriage and we'll give you the details.

To your success,
Andre Santos

Introduction

"I think we're beyond saving at this point. He wants nothing to do with me anymore."

Her husband had filed for divorce. And the more she tried to get him to see how this was a mistake, the more convinced he became that this is what he wanted.

It felt like talking to a brick wall. So she was scared to even try because she was afraid it'd just make things worse.

And that is why she almost gave up before even getting started.

We measure what we think is possible in completely irrational ways. We'll look at what we've already been able to do to determine what is possible.

A thousand years ago, flying was impossible.

Speaking to someone in a different part of the country was impossible.

Even flipping a switch to light up the room was impossible.

So even if she didn't know it… When Heather wanted to quit, it was because she'd been conditioned by everyone else who'd told her her entire life that "it takes two to tango". And that if he's not willing to work on things, there's nothing she could do.

They were wrong.

And Heather and her husband not only ripped the divorce papers to shreds, but they're more in love today, and their relationship is stronger today than it's ever been.

This was a huge surprise to her family, who thought the situation was hopeless, her marriage counselor, who had given up on her being able to reconcile… and to Heather herself.

But I knew she could get him back from the moment she told me about how stubborn and uncooperative he is.

How?

Because I've personally coached hundreds of people just like Heather, who were battling for the marriage alone, to save their marriages and families.

Just like this one:

> Things continue to improve day by day with ▮ and for those of you who don't know, less than a year ago I was preparing myself for a divorce. ▮ has now turned to me as his person to find support and share everything with me. He is asking for advice with problems that are going on with work and how I would handle certain situations. This never used to happen! I have been reciprocating with going to him for support and advice and it is making our bond even stronger.
>
> Intimacy has never been stronger, not only romantically but emotionally as well. He is opening up so much more about how he is feeling. I have stopped bottling up my feelings as well and talk to ▮ immediately when something is bothering me. We even had a very lengthy discussion about the affair and how it happened and why it happened. And it was a very calm and even loving conversation. We came out of that conversation with a clear picture of what happened to us and how we let ourselves get to the point, and how we never want to get to again.
>
> The playfulness that had been absent for so long is back and so much stronger. We laugh all the time! We are there for each other 100%. I have my husband back but even better than it ever was before!!! ▮ also has his happy loving wife back but better than before!!
>
> I can't thank Andre and Mia enough for all the help and guidance. I am 100% positive that I would be divorced right now if I hadn't found you guys!

Because we understand that the brain is a computer.

It's an incredibly complex computer with feelings - but a computer nonetheless.

Everyone is still trying to communicate with their spouses the same way my grandmother interacts with her computer... By randomly smashing the keyboard and then getting frustrated that nothing works.

What we did was study what button does what in the brain - and mapped out a system that our clients use to change how their spouse feels about them.

Because while everyone else depends on how the spouse feels - our clients can change how the spouse feels. And so they depend on nothing but their implementation of this system.

And that's how they're turning even the most stubborn, cold, and distant people into romantic and doting partners.

> Told james and tears were prickling in my eyes, james pulled me in for a huge hug and didnt let go until I was ready. Who is this man? I havent seen this man for years.❤️❤️

And that's what I want you to learn in this book.

You can stop feeling powerless and finally grab the wheel on the fate of your life and marriage.

And instead of banging your head against the wall, watching them pull further and further away every time you try to convince them to stay…

You can plant the right seeds, flip some switches in their brain, and then sit back and let their new emotions do the work for you.

Because if you try to change their mind, they'll resist you. But if you change their heart first, their mind will follow naturally.

And you'll learn the switches you need to flip to make that happen.

I'm so excited to share this system with you.

It's saved hundreds of relationships everyone else had given up on.

We've used it to end all kinds of affairs. From serious commitment to serial cheating.

In many cases, even our client didn't think their situation was possible to fix.

And in every single one of those cases, bar none, the relationship is better now than it was before.

This book will share exactly how this system works so you can implement it in your own relationship, and get your spouse back more in love than ever. Even if they're not currently on board.

Let's dive in.

Becoming a Relationship Jedi

Before we go over the process itself, it's important to understand who you have to become.

We simply can't continue to play small and expect miracles to happen. Especially when our marriage is teetering on the edge of an abyss.

If you want extraordinary things in your life, you have to be extraordinary.

And that means in both Character and Competence.

Our clients baffle their families when they save their relationships after everyone else had given up on them and decided it was impossible.

How?

Because they understand the importance of building both Character and Competence.

They build their Competence by learning and applying this system thoroughly. And with practice, discipline and consistency, they master it.

But the Character depends on them...

Just like your Character depends on you.

So what is the Character of a Relationship Jedi?

Coachable:

First and foremost, a Relationship Jedi knows that the results they have now, are a result of what they currently know.

They know that what they don't know is what is costing them their relationship.

And because of that, they're willing to learn.

Unshakable Belief:

A Relationship Jedi is also unshakable in their belief in their spouse's character. They know that there's a difference between who their spouse is, and how their spouse is acting.

And they firmly believe that their spouse is capable of being an amazing person for them again.

Because of that, they know that they're not fighting just for themselves, or their family... They're fighting for the spouse's sake too.

And they won't trash talk their spouse because they understand their behavior is a reflection of pain, not malice.

Commitment:

Finally, a Relationship Jedi understands that anything worth having is worth fighting for. They understand that nothing falls on their lap. And that their dream marriage is possible, but needs to be earned, not demanded.

This means they'll be committed to the process, that they'll put in the work, that they'll step out of their comfort zone, and that they'll be disciplined and consistent in their practice of the tools, so they build the marriage they want.

So if you have the Character of a Relationship Jedi. And you're committed to developing the skills to become one, I'm going to share with you exactly how to do that.

To sum it all up:

If you're looking for a proven way to save your marriage from the brink of divorce in 90 days or less…

And get your spouse to say "I love you" again so you can go back to the committed relationship you once had…

And you're ready to put in the work to become a Relationship Jedi yourself…

This training will show you how I've helped 100s of clients save their marriages without their spouses on board.

Rethinking How To Save A Struggling Marriage

Whenever people struggle with their marriage, they're exposed to lies & myths that are perpetuated by well-meaning… but ignorant sources.

This mainstream advice about what to do either doesn't work at all, or often makes things even worse.

If you've tried, or are currently doing any of these, you really want to pay attention:

1. "You just need to work on yourself".

Being more present, giving them space, going to the gym, thinking positive, reading more books, or however else we interpret the fluff advice of "work on yourself" may help you personally, but it'll do little to help your marriage.

There are resentments lodged in the relationship, right now. And that creates a broken trust that will shoot down whatever you attempt.

So what happens is that people spend months and months "working on themselves"... only for the spouse to either not care, or not even notice.

To get your spouse back, we need to reach them where it matters. The problem is most people don't know what that is... Or how to do it.

So they'll scream from the rooftops that you need to "work on yourself".

Don't listen.

That advice may be loud, it may be everywhere, but if it worked, we wouldn't have divorce rates as high as we do.

Working on yourself may be a beginner's first step, but it's nowhere near the full solution.

2. Therapy alone isn't going to save your marriage.

Marriage counseling is designed around both people being 100% committed to saving things.

If your spouse isn't fully on board, there's a very good chance therapy will make things worse... In fact, I'm constantly having to undo the damage caused by therapy with my clients.

Whenever a therapist hears an Entrenched spouse saying they "don't want to be married anymore", they throw their hands up and say: "Oh well, there's nothing to be done, then. We need to get you guys divorced".

And even if they try to still counsel you, they can't be simultaneously supportive of two opposing views, which inevitably makes them take sides.

Then they'll either take your side and make your spouse feel they're being ambushed... which will Entrench them further and spell major sabotage for you...

Or they'll take your spouse's side and confirm to them they're right to ask for the divorce.

3. "The Talk" never works.

Most people will try to convince their spouses to stay and give it one more chance by saying things like:

"I want us to be able to make amends",
"Are you seriously walking away from everything we've built?",
"We have to do what's best for the kids",
"I'm fighting for this marriage",
"We've been married for XX years",
"I'll always love you",
"So what, you're just giving up?",
"I did X for you!", etc...

All of these examples are routinely used by people who are desperate to change their spouse's mind... but all they do is push them even further away.

There's a lecturing undertone to them, which makes them feel you don't understand where they're coming from. This further confirms to them they need to leave this relationship quick.

If you do Communication right, you don't need your spouse's help to change how they feel about you.

4. Don't bend the knee.

We don't want to be confrontational, but we can't just bend over and ask for a spanking either.

It's very common for people to concede and start making promises on how they'll change, and giving their spouses space, because they feel they have no other option other than to do whatever the spouse says they want... but not delivering on what they need.

When we go to the doctor, we can't tell them what bug we caught. All we can do is tell them our symptoms. It is then up to the doctor to identify what the cause might be, and then based on that prescribe the treatment.

With our spouse it's the same. All they can tell you are the symptoms. So if you go along with giving them space because they asked for it, there will never be enough space that you can give them to heal the cause of the problem... Because there's no amount of fanning the smoke that will ever put out the fire.

Another big problem with this "bend the knee" approach is that it massively drops your Social Value... which, there's a reason no one wanted to buy Bitcoin when it was $13.

These approaches are based on either hoping the spouse changes their mind by themselves (not gonna happen), or trying to force them to change their mind.

This is unrealistic.

They'll either just maintain their trajectory as normal... Or double down on it to overcome whatever adversity you're creating for them.

This book aims to provide a new, simple, and faster approach to changing how your spouse feels about the relationship without creating additional adversity.

It will challenge common misconceptions and offer strategies to effectively address the underlying issues in your marriage.

Because by understanding what truly matters to your spouse and implementing effective communication techniques, you can work towards saving your marriage in a more efficient and impactful way.

Chapter takeaways:

- Working on yourself alone is not enough to save your marriage. While personal growth is important, it won't necessarily fix the underlying issues in your relationship. Simply focusing on yourself without addressing the resentments and broken trust within the marriage won't be enough to get your spouse back.
- Therapy alone may not be effective if your spouse is not fully committed. Traditional marriage counseling assumes both partners are dedicated to saving the relationship. If your spouse is not on board, therapy might even make things worse. Therapists may take sides or even recommend divorce, which can further entrench your spouse's decision.
- "The Talk" and bending the knee won't bring the desired results either. Attempts to convince your spouse to stay and make amends through emotional pleas or promises often push them further away. Lecturing or conceding to their demands without addressing the underlying issues won't lead to lasting change. It's important to find more

effective ways of communication that can positively influence their feelings towards the relationship.

> I feel like a baby in this program, but I just thought I'd say that my experience with marriage counseling has not been good at all. I feel like it is kinda playing with fire because counselors are so different and every counselor I've spoken with over the last year (& I've seen at least 6 different counselors over the last 9 months) has implied or said outright that if my husband doesn't want the marriage there's nothing I can do about it. 😳😡👎
>
> My thoughts (and it looks like maybe your husband's text is showing that it will work this way) is that this program will probably be much more beneficial than marriage counseling.

▬▬▬ to Everyone   08:50 PM

SS: Therapy put me in the victim roll even harder Andre. That's how it got worse. That shift was so powerful. Things are just clicking like a puzzle.

▬▬▬ to Everyone   08:41 PM

JW: this has helped me so much more than therapy.

The Science of Connection

"You can't make someone fall in love with you". I can't count the amount of times I've heard this...

What's worse is that most people actually believe it... Which makes no sense to me because you've made your spouse fall in love with you before, or you wouldn't be here.

Yes, you absolutely can make someone fall in love with you - in fact - you're the only one who can!

You've done it before. Even if you don't know how.

But that wasn't something your spouse decided. They didn't talk themselves into falling in love with you. It "just happened".

And it happened because of what you did, said, and made them feel.

We are NOT in control of how <u>we</u> feel about someone.

But we ARE in control over how <u>others</u> feel about us.

What generally lacks in people who say "you can't make someone fall in love with you" is the know-how to do it. So what they mean to say is "I don't know how to make my spouse fall in love with me", which is a very different problem to solve.

When this clicks for us, two big shifts take place in our brain:

- The first is that we stop blaming our spouse for how they feel - and even what they're doing. Because they're not in control of how they feel and they don't want to feel this way either.
- The second is that we stop feeling at their mercy. And realize that we have all the power to fix this - if we only learn how to change their feelings towards us.

Because, yes - you CAN break through your spouse's stubbornness, build trust back, get them to fall madly in love with you, and recommit fully to the relationship.

We simply need to pull the right levers in their brain to make it happen.

However, the way most people do it is by shooting in the dark and hoping something works. That's why they often end up doing more damage and then complaining it can't be done.

What we need isn't luck, because luck is a fickle thing. What we need is a scientific approach that can get us closer to our spouse 100% of the time.

And that means we can't rely on Psychology alone. Psychology is great, but it's easily the most subjective of sciences - and we need more than just feelings alone.

So what is the right system?

What we do is we combine Psychology and Engineering. This is a unique approach that's never been done before. It allows us to change how your spouse feels about you with AAALMOST 100% accuracy.

Because we're not just talking about feelings.

We're studying how their mind is engineered.

And this is what I call the Science of Connection.

Imagine you had a super-calculator where you could input their entire mind. Their feelings, beliefs, memories and experiences, decision-making processes, personality traits, values, pains, fears, traumas, preferences, fantasies, insecurities, ambitions, and everything else in between…

And then we could use that to calculate and anticipate how they'll think, feel, and act.

We're not just able to understand what's happening in your spouse's psychology at a level that's simply never been done before… We're also able to influence and change it.

And no, you don't have to be an engineer, or even worry about the math involved… because that's already built into the system. I did that so you don't have to.

In fact, once you get how simple this system is, you'll probably be mad how no one else was able to come up with it before.

We work with 100 clients a year, and we teach them this system so they can use it in their marriages.

We're taking people off the road to divorce, and putting them back on the path to their happily ever-after.

So how does this system work?

And how do you use it to get assured, mathematically precise results with your spouse - in the least possible amount of time?

Here are the steps…

1. You start seeing the Matrix in your relationship.

There's a technique you can use to effectively read your spouse's mind. So you can collect all the data you need for your super-calculator, without your spouse having to communicate to you how they feel. And this'll give you the boxes you need to tick in their brain to get them to forgive you, commit to you, and fall back in love with you.

2. You go through a quick Neural Makeover.

It doesn't have to take more than 12 minutes to rewire your brain out of the bad thought-patterns and habits that led to the breakdown of the relationship. There are specific processes anyone can do to shed traumas, hurts and insecurities permanently… without needing to spend 6 months in therapy. This gives you control over the person you want to be, so you become the version of you your spouse can't resist.

3. Dig them out of their Entrenchment.

You send highly specific texts to your spouse to break through their resistance. This gets them trusting you again, and being open to discussing more with you than just kids and logistics.

4. You remove their Thorns using a precise Communication Formula.

Thorns are issues and resentments in the marriage. And there's a specific way to communicate with them that will remove the Thorns for good. Once all Thorns are plucked, all issues are resolved... and they no longer want to end the relationship with you.

5. You get them to chase you by adding irresistible amounts of Social Value to the relationship.

You start building the relationship from the ground up based on the new & upgraded person you are. The overwhelming amount of Social Value you add to the relationship now makes it so you're the prize. Which means they're the ones chasing you. And this effectively solidifies in their mind that you're irresistible to them.

6. You make them fall in love with you by fulfilling their Prime Directives.

Prime Directives are the criteria for your spouse to fall in love with you. Once you identify & fulfill them, they can't help but to fall in love with you, and you shouldn't be surprised if they start worshiping the ground you walk on.

7. You get them to level up for you using Psychological Qualification.

So you stealthily train them on how to show up better for you. You then deploy these strategies whenever you need them to course correct and keep your marriage from derailing ever again.

We call it the Science of Connection because it's a literal breakdown of everything that needs to happen to reconnect you with your spouse.

Of course that your friends and family will think you must have used some kind of Jedi mind trick… That you used the Force to change your spouse's mind because they never would have thought this was possible.

But you'll know the truth.

You'll know that your success comes from the implementation of the steps in this Science of Connection.

And you'll have the knowledge of this powerful science with you for whenever you need it.

So let's walk through how to do this step-by-step now.

P.S. - if you'd like to go even deeper on this process, you can also join our private group on Facebook ("Science of Connection Global")

Chapter Takeaways:

1. Contrary to the common belief, you can influence someone's feelings towards you and make them fall in love with you again. By understanding their emotions and using scientific principles, you can rekindle their love and commitment to the relationship.
2. By combining the knowledge of human psychology with the precision of engineering techniques and scientific principles, you can develop a systematic approach to understanding your partner's emotions and influence their feelings towards you.

3. There's a well-structured step-by-step system that can guide you in transforming your relationship. This includes understanding your spouse's mind, undergoing a neural makeover to rewire your own sabotaging thought patterns, breaking through their resistance, resolving issues and resentments, adding Social Value to the relationship, fulfilling their Prime Directives, and using Psychological Qualification to level up how they're showing up in the relationship. By implementing these steps, you can transform your relationship and create a stronger and more loving connection.

Step 1 - Decoding Your Spouse's Matrix

The first step to fix anything is to be able to accurately diagnose what the real problem is, and what we need to fix. Otherwise, we'll get stuck in the hamster wheel, spinning our wheels, doing a lot of busywork... but making no progress.

The 3 big problems with getting this information is that:

1. Your spouse may not be open to communicating that to you

A lot of people get stumped here because they're operating under the myth that: *"We need them to communicate with us for us to understand them".*

The thing is… The opposite is also true: <u>They need to feel understood for them to communicate with us</u>.

This creates a chicken and the egg problem. We can't make them feel understood, so they don't let us understand them.

That means we need a way in to break that vicious cycle and turn it around.

A way to understand them without them having to open up - so we can make them feel understood right off the bat.

2. Your spouse lacks the self-awareness to be able to communicate that clearly to you

They can point out the fever, the skin rash, the abdominal pain, etc… They can't say "This is the cancer I have".

We can always communicate our symptoms, but not the causes.

Similarly, they can say they "love you, but aren't in love with you", that you don't understand them and never have, that they need space to figure things out, etc…

But they can't tell you why their feelings changed, why small things are bothering them so much now, why they have nothing left in their tank, or why they're more attracted to someone else, etc…

3. Your own emotion will serve as a bias that will filter and distort information

For instance, if you're scared there's no hope, you're liable to say they're being selfish, narcissistic, or going through a midlife crisis.

Neither of those accounts for how your spouse may have felt you pull away and become emotionally unavailable over time.

Or how that added more and more pressure and expectations on them, until at one point the relationship felt like a job…

Until one day they asked themselves if this is what's in store for them for the rest of their lives, and they couldn't shake that question out of their head.

This kept building more and more pressure until one day something snapped, and they realized they're not getting any younger... and that if they want to have any hope of being happy, they need to get out of this relationship ASAP.

Instead, it's much easier to say they're having a midlife crisis. But saying that gives us no clarity.

Whereas if we understand their emotional experience, we can identify that - in this example, the tumor we have to excise is simply the pressure and expectations that caused the problem in the first place.

What we need to know to be able to fix any marriage is:

- **Their Prime Directives** (the needs that, once fulfilled, make them fall in love)
- **Their Thorns** (the hurts that are leading to their resentment)
- **Their Fears** (the real motivations why they feel they need to walk away)
- **Their Beliefs** (about you, the relationship, and if applicable, the affair partner)
- **The types of Trust that were broken** (we'll need to know specifically which type was broken, so we can mend it)

These are the 5 Levers we'll need to pull to change how they perceive you and feel about you at a fundamental level.

Every person is different, so there isn't a one-size-fits-all approach to saving a marriage. But with the information we get from these 5

Levers, we're able to customize your approach... and craft your communication to speak to the deepest parts of your spouse's core.

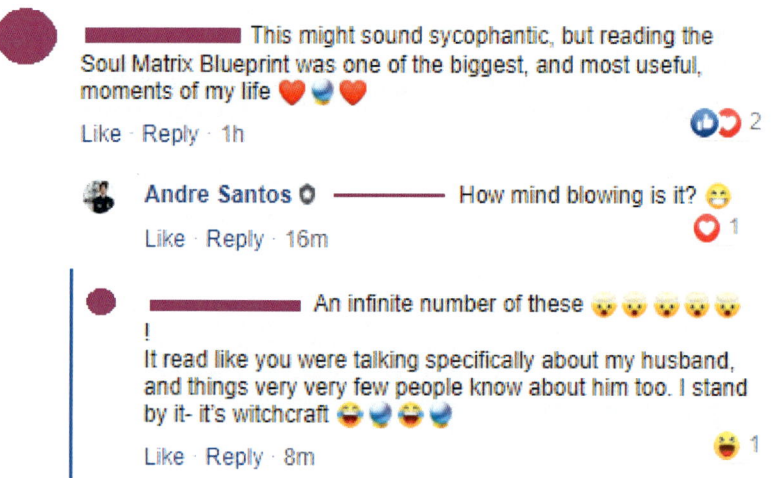

Example:

For instance, if they're "get shit done" people, there's a good chance their Prime Directive is Power. In that case - and based on that alone - we know that what they'll need more than anything else is to feel faith in themselves and in their ability to overcome problems through sheer force of will.

Knowing that, we know why they're being so stubborn and confrontational. As well as exactly what we need to be making them feel.

We also know that we can't be submissive, or they won't respect you. And that your conversations will need to be short and precise until you're back in a good place. In this case, trying to have drawn out talks about emotions will massively backfire...

Notice that we don't need that much information to know what needs to happen to fulfill their deepest needs.

And when you're a master at providing their Prime Directives, they won't be able to get enough of you.

> I've been doing the SMB tonight- OH MY GOD, it's had me in tears.
> The Power section is EXACTLY ▬▬, especially the parts about what can happen when they lose faith in themselves- it sooooooo accurately describes him while I was ill. I never really thought about it, but that was exactly what happened to him. I've even thought over the past few months, should I try for him still, when he got so controlling and was always taking over by the end, do I really want that back. But he hadn't been like that for the 8 years before, just the few months before he left, so I should have realised that wasn't really 'him'.
> It's honestly really upset me tonight, reading it and opening my eyes to so much!
> Do you mind me asking, is the SMB a general psychological thing, or something you've developed? Some of the things you say are like witchcraft they're so spot on, but the SMB is a whole other level!

The problem is that to uncover this information, we need to go deeper than what they'll be able to share.

So how do we pop open the hood and read their mind without them needing to say a word to us?

Well, when it comes to Prime Directives and Trust Types, we can observe those directly in their behavior.

Prime Directives:

To identify their Prime Directives, you need to watch out for these personality traits to figure out what quadrant they're in:

🔥 Power:

People under this quadrant are very "get shit done", they're often more on the impulsive side, and constantly seek to prove themselves. They can come off aggressive, though…

💙 Love:

People under this quadrant are big proponents of communication, they're sensitive and tend to be dreamers. They're also excellent manipulators if they feel slighted.

📚 Knowledge:

These are the people who thrive in organizing and cataloging. They tend to come across as party-poopers, though, since they're often the ones to point out where the problems lie. They're also masters of the silent treatment, and easily ghost at the drop of a hat.

💡 Wisdom:

These are the innovators and creators. They're constantly coming up with ideas and get deeply invested in them. If you get on their bad side, though, they're experts at making people feel dumb.

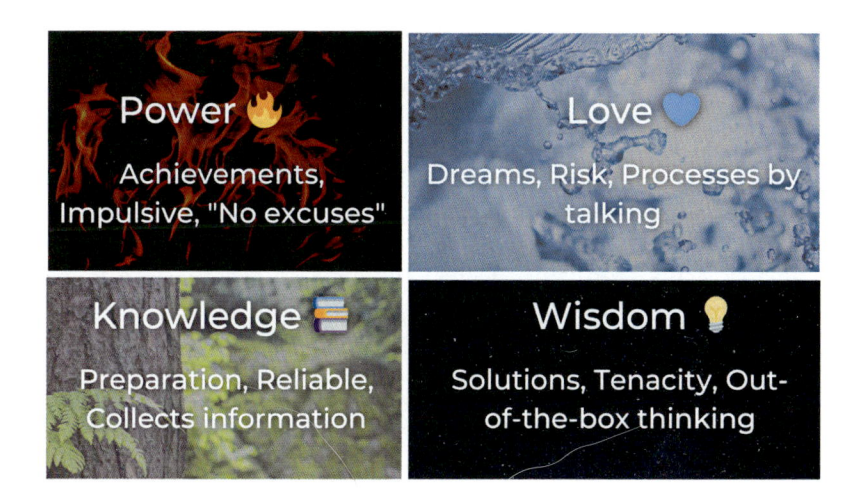

Power 🔥 Achievements, Impulsive, "No excuses"	**Love** 💙 Dreams, Risk, Processes by talking
Knowledge 📚 Preparation, Reliable, Collects information	**Wisdom** 💡 Solutions, Tenacity, Out-of-the-box thinking

Take a minute now to identify what you think your spouse's Prime Directive quadrant is and write it down on a piece of paper. (If you're unsure between them, pick the two that most control their behavior - they often work together in a matrix).

We'll make use of this information later to flip those switches in their brain that will get them to fall in love with you!

Once that's done, we need to identify which Trust Types are broken and write those down too.

Specifically, write down which of these have been breached. It can just be two... Or it might be all five.

Trust Types:

Vulnerability Trust - They don't trust you with their emotions, they don't open up and don't care to entertain any conversation about the relationship.

Intention Trust - They don't trust your intentions. They're automatically resistant to anything you have to say, may have accused you of being manipulative, or that you only care about yourself.

Sovereign Trust - They don't trust that you trust them to make decisions. They have to assert themselves, oftentimes in an aggressive manner, and may have accused you of being controlling.

Privacy Trust - They don't trust you with sensitive information. This will be breached if you go through their phone, or disclose details of your relationship with friends or family without their permission. They'll feel exposed, and this will turn to resentment towards you.

Physical Trust - They don't trust you with their safety. They fear you might cause them harm, or that you're unable to protect them from harm. Banging a door, or having an anger outburst is often enough to trigger this at an unconscious level. This is more common with women, but not exclusive.

You can learn more about Trust Types in our private Facebook group ("Science of Connection Global").

Thorns, Fears, and Beliefs:

When it comes to identifying their Thorns, Fears, and Beliefs, the main thing we need to make peace with, is that our POV isn't useful...

We already know it. And if we stay locked in that, we're stuck with only 50% of the picture.

That's why we need to put ourselves in our spouse's shoes and observe the situation as if we were them.

This is what we call the Clairvoyance Exercise.

This allows us to see from their perspective, to feel their emotions, to think their thoughts. We can then use all this in communication with them.

When our clients do this with their spouses, their jaws hit the floor. They never would have imagined how deeply our clients understand them. And that alone, is often enough to make them feel more loved than any amount of words or romantic gestures.

This is also how I'm able to talk to my clients and lay out exactly what their spouse is thinking, feeling, and even what they'll do... Without even having had a single conversation with them.

My clients often say it's like witchcraft because it's so accurate. It's not witchcraft. It's science.

And if I can do this without even meeting them... with people who were stubborn as an ox, struggling with depression, PTSD, midlife crisis, who refused to open up or disclose any of their emotions... then you can do this too with your spouse.

This exercise isn't just great for giving you the information you need... A lot of my clients find this process highly therapeutic as well.

> Clairvoyance, to put yourself in your spouse's shoes, for more than a second is a really good exercise. And, to say to your spouse you have my permission to control my brain/thoughts is a great illustration on the other side. If you're (me) obsessing over what he's thinking or why he's not doing something- he has control. Do the clairvoyance first and I bet you can let it go - that obsession. Let go for a while (I'm telling myself this) bc the thinking and double-thinking of his possible thoughts is driving me nuts.

In fact, you'll know you've been successful when you think to yourself that if you were in their position, there's a good chance you would have done the same...

It's not to say they're right to do it. It's that you feel compassion for the deeper emotions that led them to act in the ways that they did.

If we don't go that deep because we're scared of what we'll see, we'll never go deep enough to make them feel understood.

This is why it's important to heal our own pains and resentments... because we can't pick up their lens if we're not willing to put ours down for a minute first.

Chapter takeaways:

- To fix any marriage, it is crucial to accurately diagnose the underlying problems. This requires going beyond surface-level communication and identifying the Prime Directives, Thorns, Fears, Beliefs, and Trust Types that have been broken for your spouse. These five levers will help you understand and address the core issues in your relationship.
- Your spouse may not be open to communicating their needs and feelings, lack self-awareness to express themselves clearly, or you might be influenced by your own emotional biases. To break this cycle, it is important to find alternative ways to understand your spouse without relying only on their direct communication. Fortunately, we can identify their Prime Directives and broken Trust Types through observation alone.
- To truly understand your spouse's Thorns, Fears, and Beliefs, it is essential to let go of your own perspective and have compassion for their deeper emotions. The Clairvoyance exercise, where you put yourself in your spouse's shoes and observe the situation from their perspective, can help you gain deeper insights into their emotions and thoughts. This requires healing your own pains and resentments to approach the situation with

empathy and a willingness to see things from their point of view.

Step 2 - Go through a fast Neural Makeover

"Working on yourself" is trendy on social media... but in practice, the message it sends to your spouse is that they were right to break up with you, and "you're welcome".

Another huge problem with this "work on yourself" advice is the lack of clarity.

What does it mean, and what does one do to "work on themselves"?

Popular choices include:

Striving for a better work-life balance,
Working out,
Eating cleaner,
Reading books,
Doing yoga,
Journaling,
Therapy,
Etc...

...but the possibilities are endless.

The thing all those strategies have in common, though, is that while they're generally good things that you should do for yourself... they're not the root cause of what went wrong in the relationship. And they don't help your spouse fulfill their Prime Directives.

That means that relying on these things to save the relationship is like wanting to fix a broken car with a fresh coat of paint.

If we're brutally honest for a moment and we observe the roots of the problems in the relationship... you'll be at the center as either the person who caused it, or the person who didn't stop it.

This isn't to make you feel bad, because it wasn't your fault.

Sure, your spouse will blame you... You may even blame yourself; but if there was a car crash, who do you blame?

The car, or the driver?

Assuming the car is functioning, most people would blame the driver.

Well, if your Unprocessed Emotional Tension was driving the car, then it's not your fault for crashing.

Unprocessed Emotional Tension are the fears, traumas, insecurities, and negative emotions we accumulate over a lifetime...

And when we stack these tensions on top of our stress and responsibilities, it can manifest in many ways:

- **Distress:**

Being short, snappy, tense around our spouse and having little patience for delays, mistakes, or their emotions. Our Unprocessed

Emotional Tension will then come out in what's infamously referred to as: "the tone".

This makes our spouse feel we're angry at them. That makes them defensive, and starts creating resentments and feelings of unfairness... which inevitably grow into Thorns.

- **Stoicism:**

A deep seated fear and inability to connect with our emotions (may feel like a persistent sense of apathy).

This makes the spouse feel alone and unsupported, because they can't seem to connect with you emotionally. This makes them feel insecure in themselves...

And eventually, as a defense mechanism, they start to resent you instead. The Thorns strengthen at this point when they convince themselves you're just not capable of connecting (they're wrong!)

- **Fragility:**

Being on the edge of breaking down emotionally and feeling we have little control over our emotions.

This makes the spouse feel they're responsible for your every emotion. And after some time they start walking on eggshells. No matter what they do, or what they try, "there's no winning with you".

In time, they start shifting their focus away from themselves and more onto you. At that point, they'll blame you for putting them in those situations, which is a common source of Thorns for the relationship.

This level of self-awareness is often scary and uncomfortable, but necessary if we're to change it.

When we go with the "working on yourself" approach, we often just mask & suppress our fears and insecurities, which kicks the can on the problem.

You can "fake it till you make it" for 5 minutes; but relationships are built on what we're doing unconsciously. When you're not paying attention, how will you sound? How will you come across?

If our Unprocessed Emotional Tensions go unattended, we'll end up in the same situation. We'll re-cause the same problems in the relationship because we didn't change the roots of how we add to it.

What we need is genuine healing that eliminates your insecurities. Not by trying to think or affirm your way out of your emotions, but by rewiring how they are coded in your neurology.

It's kind of like deleting your phone's cache to make it run smoother.

That means you effortlessly become the version of you that your spouse fell in love with. Confident, easy to be around, and more efficient in coping with stress.

Not to mention you're able to resolve future problems and emotions easily... so they don't strain your relationship once it's rebuilt.

Your Neural Makeover isn't just for the longevity of the relationship after you save it, though... It's fundamental for the process of rebuilding it itself.

<u>Because the actual process of rebuilding the marriage only starts after we finish this step.</u>

You'll only be able to make your spouse feel at ease when you're in a state of emotional harmony and a natural, effortless confidence.

Then you can apply the next steps of the process without carrying the vibe of Distress, Stoicism, or Fragility.

So the actual rebuilding of the relationship process ONLY STARTS after you are the one driving the car... and your emotions are safely secured on the baby seat in the back.

This is another reason "Work on yourself" is terrible advice... It's like having a risotto recipe where the only step listed is to turn on the stove.

Time is always working against you through the process of getting your spouse back.

So we need to make sure we do this healing process as quickly as possible.

Which is why I do not recommend talk therapy, CBT, EMDR, hypnotherapy, or any therapeutic model that requires more than a single session to permanently heal your traumas & insecurities.

And yes, it can be that fast.

Having a broken door knob for 35 years doesn't mean it'll take 35 years to fix it.

For example, one of my clients, Ben, owns a catering business, works crazy hours... which on top of all the Unprocessed Emotional Tensions from his life, packed him with a lot of Distress.

Naturally, this came across to his wife... and was one of the main causes of the Thorns in their relationship that led to her asking for the divorce.

Ben arranged his schedule so he had a single free afternoon... and that's when he worked through our Neural Makeover Tools.

His wife's demeanor towards him softened literally the moment he came down the stairs.

From there, he applied the rest of the steps, and now they're happily in love and recommitted to one another.

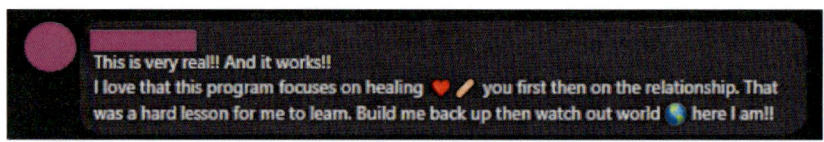

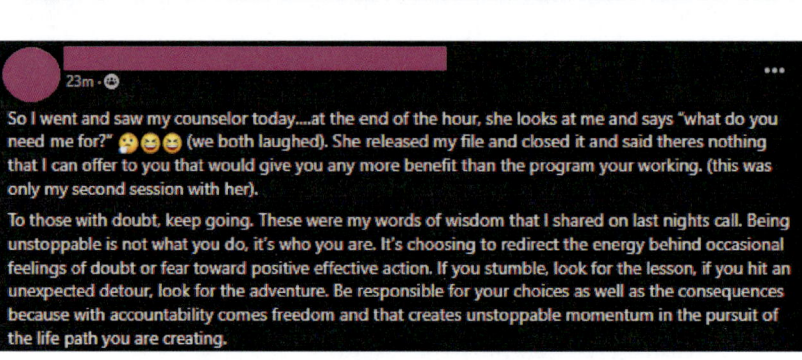

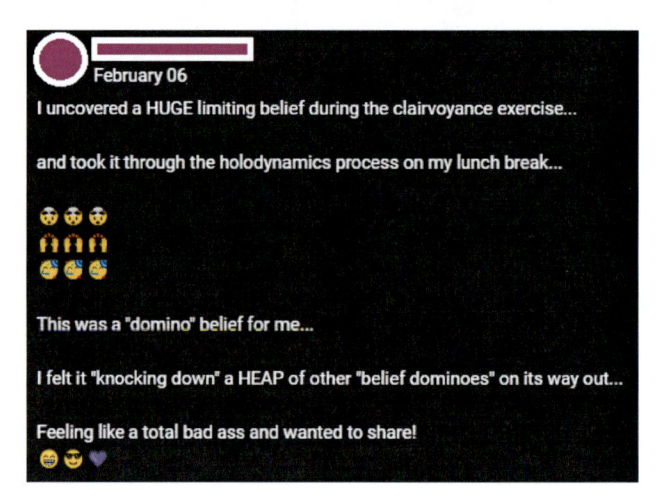

> This is very real!! And it works!!
> I love that this program focuses on healing ❤️ ✏️ you first then on the relationship. That was a hard lesson for me to learn. Build me back up then watch out world 🌍 here I am!!

> 23m · 😊
>
> So I went and saw my counselor today.....at the end of the hour, she looks at me and says "what do you need me for?" 🤪😂😅 (we both laughed). She released my file and closed it and said theres nothing that I can offer to you that would give you any more benefit than the program your working. (this was only my second session with her).
>
> To those with doubt, keep going. These were my words of wisdom that I shared on last nights call. Being unstoppable is not what you do, it's who you are. It's choosing to redirect the energy behind occasional feelings of doubt or fear toward positive effective action. If you stumble, look for the lesson, if you hit an unexpected detour, look for the adventure. Be responsible for your choices as well as the consequences because with accountability comes freedom and that creates unstoppable momentum in the pursuit of the life path you are creating.

> February 06
>
> I uncovered a HUGE limiting belief during the clairvoyance exercise...
>
> and took it through the holodynamics process on my lunch break...
>
> 🤯🤯🤯
> 🙏🙏🙏
> 🥳🥳🥳
>
> This was a "domino" belief for me...
>
> I felt it "knocking down" a HEAP of other "belief dominoes" on its way out...
>
> Feeling like a total bad ass and wanted to share!
> 😁😍💜

Chapter takeaways:

- The popular advice of "working on yourself" doesn't address the root causes of the problems in your relationship. While self-improvement activities like maintaining work-life balance, exercising, or therapy have their benefits, they may not directly address the core issues that led to the breakdown in the relationship or help fulfill your spouse's Prime Directives.
- Unprocessed Emotional Tension, which includes fears, traumas, insecurities, and negative emotions accumulated over a lifetime, can manifest in various ways within a relationship. It can lead to distress, stoicism, or fragility, all of which can create a sense of anger, disconnection, or insecurity in your spouse. These unresolved emotional tensions can contribute to the development of Thorns in the relationship.
- Instead of simply masking or suppressing fears and insecurities, genuine healing involves rewiring how these emotions are coded in your neurology. By addressing and resolving these emotional tensions, you can become the version of yourself that your spouse initially fell in love with. This healing process is crucial for rebuilding the relationship and creating emotional harmony, confidence, and resilience that will support the subsequent steps in the process to rebuild the relationship.

I still can't get over how much I've changed, and the fact I wanted to skip the first few levels because 'I don't need them'... 🙈🙈
It's been the absolute most important thing for me- to deal with situations as they are, rather than feel out of control and at the mercy of them- and I think my different energy/ attitude is probably the most important thing for how things with ▬▬▬ have changed too- if the person who wrote that first snapshot begged me back, I'd probably run for the hills too 😅😅

😅 1

Step 3 - Dig them out of their Entrenchment

Now that you're back to your most badass self, we can start the process to get them to fall back in love with us.

But before we're able to do that, the very first thing we need to do is to get them out of their state of Entrenchment.

Entrenchment is a state of hyper-defensiveness where it doesn't matter what you say, or what you try... they only dig in deeper into their anti-relationship stance.

This is caused by Thorns that have been left festering too long. At that point your spouse no longer trusts you, your intentions, or anything you have to say.

It's completely normal to feel powerless in this situation because of how stubborn they're being.

This is where most people get stuck.

Because it feels impossible to communicate with an Entrenched spouse.

And if we skip over the Disentrenchment part of the process... and try to talk to them about the relationship, our feelings, or why we need to work on the marriage BEFORE we Disentrench them... all we do is Entrench them more. 😬

Because if we have a thorn piercing our skin, it'll hurt to even touch it. And that's the fatal mistake people make constantly when trying to fix their marriage.

So how do we Disentrench your spouse?

We need to get their trust back, so they feel comfortable talking to us again.

Contrary to popular belief, trust doesn't take a long time to repair. Most of our clients go from "I never want to speak to you again!" to their spouse holding back tears as they talk about their feelings, in 1-2 weeks.

This is why we need to uncover the types of trust that were broken, as well as the beliefs they have about you in Step 1.

Because trust is simply a set of beliefs your spouse has about you. And if we know what those beliefs are, we can change them.

For example, let's say the trust that is broken is their Intention Trust. Meaning that they don't trust your intentions.

And one of their beliefs is that you are manipulative, and will say anything to get your way, but don't mean it.

If we say things like:

"I want us to be able to make amends"
"We have to do what's best for the kids"
"I forgive you"

"I'm fighting for this marriage"
"Can we work towards that?"
"We've been married for XX years"
"I'll fight for you"
"I'll always love you"
"I hear you, but..."
"What about XYZ?"
"I did X for you!"
"So what, you're just giving up?"

…you reset the clock and you're back to square one.

This is one of the reasons people struggle with Entrenchment.

Because they don't realize when they're doing and saying things like these that keep re-entrenching their spouse.

All we're doing in saying these things is reinforcing their belief that you'll manipulate and say anything to get your way.

This will Entrench them, because it's proof that you'll put your wants, feelings and opinions above theirs.

Which will only result in confirming they're right not to trust your intentions.

Instead, phrase it like:

"I can't believe I didn't even realize how [deep emotion] you were feeling... 😔
I know you'll probably just think I'm being manipulative or whatever, but could I ask you a couple of questions about this?
It's totally fine if you're not ready for that...
I just want to understand you and where you're at better."

With this phrasing, and the appropriate tonality, we start shifting their belief about you. And start rebuilding trust in your intentions. (Which in our example was the type of trust that had been broken, but adjust to whichever Trust Types are damaged in your case)

This works regardless if they're willing to talk or not... Because even if they're not, this is showing that you respect where they're at emotionally.

And this plants a seed in their neurology that we're trustworthy.

For instance, this was a client whose husband had been emotionally closed off for years. She applied these strategies with him and it was easier than she ever thought it would be to get him to open up.

And then her jaw hit the floor a few days later when suddenly he was starting conversations about his emotions.

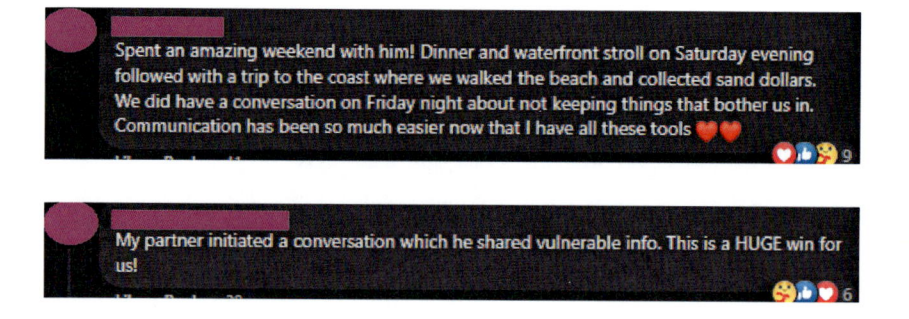

> Spent an amazing weekend with him! Dinner and waterfront stroll on Saturday evening followed with a trip to the coast where we walked the beach and collected sand dollars. We did have a conversation on Friday night about not keeping things that bother us in. Communication has been so much easier now that I have all these tools ❤️❤️
>
> ❤️👍🤗 9

> My partner initiated a conversation which he shared vulnerable info. This is a HUGE win for us!
>
> 🤗👍❤️ 6

This is also a great example of how, if we're not in control of the relationship... it's because we're not being flexible enough with our communication strategy.

<u>We always need to adapt our communication to the data we uncovered in Step 1</u>.

What if my spouse is suuuuper stubborn?

That's fine, because using this phrasing, we're not creating any opposition. There's nothing for them to resist, or be stubborn against.

If we say things like *"I did everything for you!"*, or *"Please, just give me another chance!"* then we're creating opposition, and they'll for sure be stubborn and Entrench against you.

In about 90% of cases, these are secret resentments they're not telling you about... but that will race through their mind whenever they get a message from you.

So having that clarity on the Thorns they're dealing with internally (Step 1) is your ace-in-the-hole.

Because now you can craft a message that shows them you understand them better than they know themselves.

This is the secret sauce that takes them from completely cemented in their position... and possibly ghosting you... to agreeing with you and engaging in conversation in sometimes as little as 30 seconds.

Chapter takeaways:

- Before you can effectively communicate with your spouse and work on the relationship, it's important to disentrench them from their state of hyper-defensiveness. Entrenchment occurs when trust has been broken, and your spouse no longer trusts your intentions or anything you say. Skipping the disentrenchment process and trying

to talk about the relationship or your feelings can further entrench them.
- Trust can be repaired relatively quickly if you uncover the Types of Trust that were broken and the beliefs your spouse has about you. Trust is a set of beliefs, and by understanding those beliefs, you can work on changing them. It's crucial to be mindful of the words and phrases you use, as certain statements can reinforce negative beliefs and entrench your spouse further. By phrasing your communication in a way that shows you intimately understand them and how they feel, you can start shifting their beliefs and rebuilding trust.
- Flexibility in your communication strategy is essential. It's important to adapt your communication based on the information you discovered in Step 1, when you uncovered the specific beliefs and Thorns your spouse has. By crafting messages that show you understand them better than they know themselves, you can avoid creating opposition and resistance. Instead, you can engage in conversation and move them from a position of entrenchment to agreement. Having clarity on their internal struggles and tailoring your communication accordingly can be the secret sauce to breaking through their defenses and fostering productive dialogue.

It's been so powerful! You really get it when you see it in action, don't you! 😮
She's been saying 'at last, someone gets it!', even though I haven't actually agreed with any of her negative statements! 😮 I'm in awe of these techniques! 😮 🙇‍♀️

❤️ 1

He replied straight away to say he's ok, and a big smiley again! 😊 I've never had so many smileys from him til I started getting your advice! Honestly, you must be doing witchcraft of some sort! 😂😂

Hello everyone just a quick share, the last couple weeks have been really good, my wife and I have reconnected there has been no tension, no arguing, no tone when speaking. We have been working together on some projects and it has gone smoothly. We have been intimate which hasn't been there in months. She put her wedding ring back on just 2 days ago which meant a lot to me. We have progressed forward more in the last couple weeks than we have in a very long time. I see this getting better and building back our relationship is looking better everyday. I am thankful for this group and what I have been learning. Looking forward to much more growth in the future.

Step 4 - Pluck Thorns

Now that we're able to have a conversation with them without them bolting like a jittery cat... we can start plucking those Thorns one by one until they're all gone.

There's a story I like about a lion that was terrorizing villages. He was extremely aggressive, so the townsfolk were starting to think it was a demon.

One day, a young girl disappeared from the village. And after hours of searching, the villagers found her sitting next to the lion.

The girl's father rallied some men and armed them with pitchforks and other farming utensils they could use as weapons. They were prepared to try and fight the beast.

The girl, however, was unharmed.

And the lion... much to the villagers' surprise, was relaxed even with the villagers' commotion.

The girl happily returned to her father, with a wide grin on her face. And when she approached him, she raised her hand and revealed a long bloody thorn resting on her palm.

She then proceeded to tell the villagers how she noticed the lion had this thorn in his paw.

And the pain it caused was why he was so aggressive. Once she removed it, the lion became docile towards her.

This is the same thing that happens in relationships.

It's easy for us to judge our spouse's behavior. To say they're hardly the same person they were. And get upset because they're being so mean.

That's unhelpful, though…

Much more helpful is to recognize that, like the lion, they're just in pain. And hurt people hurt people.

Hurt turns to resentment. Fear turns to hopelessness. And both turn into Thorns.

When people say things like *"I love you, but I'm not in love with you"*, *"We need to get a divorce"*, *"I deserve to be happy!"* or anything similar in which they're expressing their dissatisfaction with the relationship... what they're actually saying is that there are Thorns pricking their skin.

These Thorns hurt, and they don't know what to do to stop the pain other than to pull away.

When we remove the Thorns - which again, must be done ONLY AFTER we've disentrenched them, or it will backfire! - we're able to set a clean slate upon which to build the new relationship from the ground up.

The trick, though, and one of the biggest reasons people mess up when trying to pluck Thorns... is to not have a conversation about them!

There are no words scarier than "We need to talk".

Any attempt to have "The Talk", no matter how you phrase it, will come across as lecturing and pressure.

That will compromise trust and Re-Entrench them right back.

Instead, we want to be able to have multiple surgical conversations... Each lasting no longer than 3 minutes to pluck these Thorns without generating resistance.

A common mistake people make in these conversations is that when they apologize... they try to explain why they did what they did.

And the less responsive the spouse is, the deeper into the explanation they go.

People tend to think that if the spouse understands why they did what they did, then certainly they'd forgive them... Right?

...e problem isn't that they don't understand you, the problem ...at they don't feel understood BY you.

More than understanding why you made your mistake, they need to know that you understand how your mistake made them feel...

They won't care to even listen before then.

This is why it's important to collect the data we need on their Thorns and Fears in Step 1.

Because people think that we need communication to understand one another... when actually, the opposite is also true. We need to understand one another to communicate.

Armed with that information, there are 3 main things we need to do when we're plucking Thorns:

   1. Take responsibility for the situation... and genuinely apologize for how you either caused the problem; or failed to prevent it.

This is important because they already blame you for the situation. If you attempt to defend yourself, they'll feel unheard, and will Entrench further. They need to know you know that you are to blame.

By taking responsibility, you can get them to feel validated and understood. Do it right and they'll even step up to defend you from yourself.

   2. Phrase their feelings better than they can.

If you tell them you understand them, they'll call BS.

But if you're able to verbalize how they feel better than they can, it's undeniable that you understand them.

And that feeling of being understood is what plucks the Thorn.

Again, this is why Step 1 is fundamental. We can't make them feel understood if we don't understand them.

3. Show vulnerability in your apology.

This is crucial for them to accept the apology. The more vulnerable you are, the more believable your apology will be. And the more empathy and compassion your spouse will feel for you.

Here is an example of a Thorn Plucking conversation written by one of my clients:

> "How are you doing? Is everything okay? You seem tense
> I know you'll probably think this is way too late in the game, so you won't even want to hear it, but my lack of response toward you when we were on trips/vacations.
> I can only imagine how alone I made you feel when there were those awkward times and I didn't allow free flowing intimacy between us. You probably felt so rejected, hurt and even resentment toward me that I couldn't partner with you in the most basic but intimate way.
> I was totally selfish - only thinking of myself, isolating emotionally from you, not taking your feelings into consideration. I didn't care how you felt. I centered that all around me. But you are not to blame. It was not your fault - me rejecting you was borne out of my insecurities and lack of confidence - that I'm not engaging enough, not sexy enough, not smart enough. None of this is on you.
> I am sorry . . . I don't expect you to forgive me . . . Honestly, in your shoes, I don't think I'd forgive myself. . . . I just hope one day maybe we can move past all this . . ."

Unsurprisingly, he forgave her for that Thorn almost instantly. So she just moved on to the next one.

Here's another client who was blocked on social media and had to email her Thorn Plucking. In this case, I wrote her email with her (well… mostly for her) and she just had to hit send.

> **Author**
> Andre Santos I emailed him this today. #ididntedit He just came into my office. He said he forgives me. He said he realizes that most of my actions are a product of the environments I was in in the past. And he apologized for only hurting me more in return. We hugged it out for a while and I did shed a couple tears. (Couldn't help it)
>
> Hopefully that's a good outcome... he definitely has empathy and compassion for me now!

To say her jaw dropped at his response would be an understatement. But if we understand the boxes that need to be ticked... And we tailor our Thorn Plucking to match not only their Thorns, but their Prime Directives, Fears, Beliefs, and broken Trust Types - we can successfully pluck the Thorns every single time.

And once the Thorns are plucked, they stop pulling away from you.

Which means you're now able to reconnect with them without any more resistance.

This is where it gets fun. 😎

Chapter takeaways:

- Recognize the pain behind their behavior. Just like the lion in the story, your spouse's hurt and pain can manifest as aggressive or hurtful behavior. It's important to understand that hurt people hurt people. Instead of judging their behavior, try to recognize that they're in pain and dealing with Thorns that are causing them distress.
- Once you've disentrenched your spouse and gained their trust, you can start addressing the Thorns in the relationship. These Thorns represent the underlying issues and hurts that need to be addressed. However, it's crucial to avoid having a single, overwhelming conversation about

the Thorns if they're not initiating one themselves. Instead, have multiple surgical conversations, each lasting no longer than 3 minutes, to pluck the Thorns without generating resistance.
- When addressing the thorns, it's important to take responsibility for the situation and genuinely apologize for your role in causing or failing to prevent the problem. Additionally, you should strive to phrase their feelings better than they can and show vulnerability in your apology. By understanding their emotions and demonstrating vulnerability, you can help them feel validated, understood, and more open to accepting your apology.

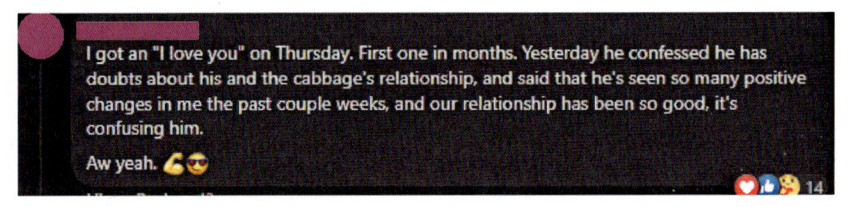

> I got an "I love you" on Thursday. First one in months. Yesterday he confessed he has doubts about his and the cabbage's relationship, and said that he's seen so many positive changes in me the past couple weeks, and our relationship has been so good, it's confusing him.
>
> Aw yeah. 💪😎
>
> ❤️👍🤗 14

*Cabbage = Affair Partner

Step 5 - Get them to chase you

Now that we've removed the Thorns that were driving them away from us, it's important we stop chasing them.

Removing the Thorns first is crucial for this. Otherwise they won't chase you no matter what you do, because they don't want to get pricked.

But once that's done, what we need to do is to get them to chase us. That's the only way to have a healthy and fulfilling relationship that can easily last a lifetime.

Not to mention this makes the rest of the process almost effortless... because they'll be the ones doing most of the work to get your attention.

Think of it this way…

Humans are mammals. And aside from a prefrontal cortex, our brain isn't all that different from a dog's.

Our limbic system works exactly the same. And if you have a dog, or have ever interacted with a dog, you know that if you chase a dog, the dog runs away.

They can't help themselves. That instinct is rooted in the most primal areas of the brain and will override their behavior.

Every. Single. Time.

Humans are the same. If you're chasing your spouse, their instinct - that will override their conscious thought and intention... is to pull back.

Keep chasing them, and you'll chase them away.

If you want the dog to come to you, all you have to do is hold out a piece of bacon, and it'll come running.

So what's the crispy bacon that will get your spouse running towards you?

Social Value.

You can think of Social Value as an invisible metric your spouse has of you (and everyone else).

This is what tells them how much time they want to spend with you, how much respect they have for you, and how attracted they are to you.

Social Value is why rock stars have groupies. And you can create that same effect with your spouse. 😉

When you chase your spouse, you're communicating your Social Value is lower than theirs. They are the prize that you are chasing.

This has an immediate effect in those primal areas of their brain that kicks in the instinct to pull away from you.

Because if your Social Value is lower than theirs, they'd be settling in being with you. And no one wants to settle.

The more needy you come across, like begging them to stay... the worse the disparity in Social Value, and the more repelling your efforts will be.

Be mindful that not chasing them isn't enough. If all you do is not chase the dog, it'll just go towards the nearest food it can smell.

> She's starting to chase me more! Mentions future plans of living together and told me to show more affection in public to her!!

We have to increase your Social Value in their eyes, so they can't resist you.

And, counter-intuitively to what we might think... Even if it will impress strangers, your status, wealth, and appearance will matter very little to your spouse...

These are superficial, and your spouse needs more in a life-partner.

So here are a few examples of how to gain irresistible Social Value for your spouse:

1. Influencing, instead of being influenced by their mood

If you follow them into a bad mood, then they're in control of your emotional state. And you show them they have more Social Value than you do.

If you're bubbly and ignore their bad mood, they feel alone... and may distrust you because your positivity won't feel genuine.

The trick is to adjust to where they are, but not follow them down the rabbit hole... and then pull them into a better mood with you.

For instance, if they're stressed and upset about something from work. Instead of getting upset and stressed back, you step into a place of support and curiosity. You give them a space to vent, you become their rock while they release the tension from the day. When the tension is released, you make them feel better about themselves, lighten the mood, and help them relax...

This shows you're the one who sets the environment, but from a very respectful and compassionate place. They're following you with no resistance at all... and they want to continue to follow you because you're so great at making them feel better - Instant Social Value boost.

And this can happen insanely fast.

This is what one of the members of our Facebook Group experienced in her relationship immediately after she learned how to do this to flip his state.

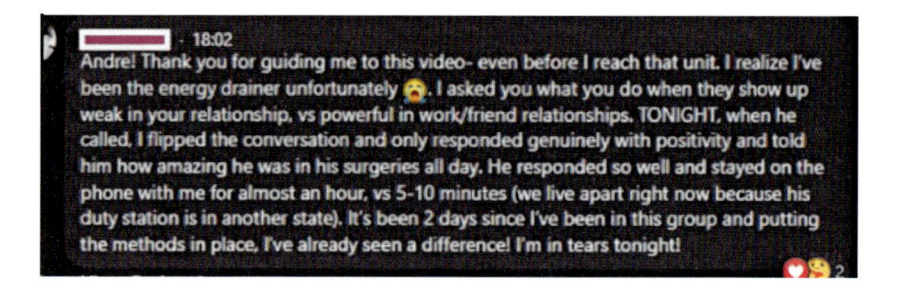

> ▬▬▬ · 18:02
> Andre! Thank you for guiding me to this video- even before I reach that unit. I realize I've been the energy drainer unfortunately 😱. I asked you what you do when they show up weak in your relationship, vs powerful in work/friend relationships. TONIGHT, when he called, I flipped the conversation and only responded genuinely with positivity and told him how amazing he was in his surgeries all day. He responded so well and stayed on the phone with me for almost an hour, vs 5-10 minutes (we live apart right now because his duty station is in another state). It's been 2 days since I've been in this group and putting the methods in place, I've already seen a difference! I'm in tears tonight!

2. Taking your time

If they take an hour to text you back, and you reply within the minute, what are you communicating about yourself?

You're demonstrating your time isn't that valuable. May even come across as though you've been sitting at the edge of your seat for the past hour waiting for their text. Not the most confident look…

If you take your time to get back to them… or even open the message, so it doesn't show 'seen'… you communicate instead that your time is valuable. And you get them checking their phone often to see when you've responded.

If they get upset, calmly let them know you were doing something and move on. This is a sign your Social Value is so far below theirs, that they'll have the expectation that you should be at their beck and call. (The only exception to this is emergencies, of course)

Get them to value your time if you want them to value you more.

3. Aligning them with their Gender Psychology

A sad but overwhelming trend that occurs in about 90% of struggling marriages… is Gender Role Reversal.

To be clear, this isn't political. This isn't about some 1950's conception of what a woman is supposed to do around the house either.

This is about biology, about our hardwiring - regardless of who makes the most money or vacuums the carpets.

What does matter, though, and is exceedingly rare… is that men feel like men - powerful and respected; and women feel like women - cherished and protected.

A lot of career women struggle to "switch it off" when they come home. And then inadvertently present themselves as masculine to their husbands.

On the other hand, men are being conditioned to be "nice guys", and genuinely believe that's what women want. Because that's what we're being told in every aspect of media.

Even when they're leaders in their company, they become followers in the home.

Whichever the trigger that starts the Reversal, it creates a negative loop where:

- The man feels weaker, and tries to please the woman
- The woman realizes he's not confident and that she can't rely on him to lead or take care of her
- The woman takes it upon herself to fill the "get shit done" role since he clearly won't
- He feels no matter what he does, he can never please her

Until…

- One of them has enough, and revolts

This is often the cause of midlife crisis, affairs, or the spouse checking out, completely out of the blue.

When we align our spouse with their Gender Psychology, they can't help but feel a primal passion and desire for you. This triggers the "You're my prize" mindset in their neurology we're looking for.

Case in point… This is what happens when you align them with their Gender Psychology:

- **Write a brief summary of how your interactions went with your spouse this week.**
  My husband is showing up consistently with warmth. He's initiating physical affection as well as letting me touch him. The touch is with meaning and tenderness. He's not taking space, he's engaging with the kids and operating more in his MGR. He's initiated "I love you a few times". There's more emotional bids occurring and reciprocated responses between us. We are also playful and sharing of the day. My husband is using words like "us" and "we". He's also making dinner for me and doing things to make my day easier. There is some light sensual touching within comfort.

MGR = Male Gender Role

When you stack multiple sources of Social Value like this, you don't have to worry about your spouse going away.

And it'll be very easy for you to get them to want to work on the relationship with you now... because they want nothing more than to please you.

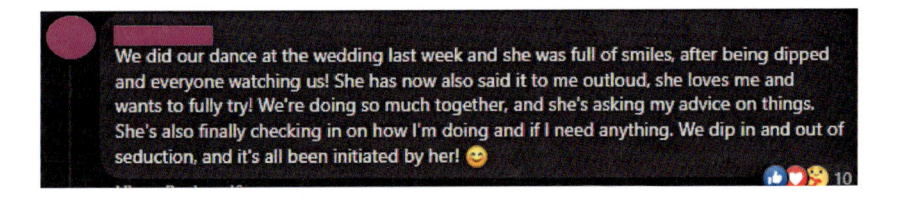

> We did our dance at the wedding last week and she was full of smiles, after being dipped and everyone watching us! She has now also said it to me outloud, she loves me and wants to fully try! We're doing so much together, and she's asking my advice on things. She's also finally checking in on how I'm doing and if I need anything. We dip in and out of seduction, and it's all been initiated by her! 😊

Chapter takeaways:

- Stop chasing and increase your Social Value. Chasing them communicates that your Social Value is lower than theirs, which can trigger their instinct to pull away. Instead, focus on increasing your Social Value in their eyes. This can be done by influencing their mood, taking your time to respond to them, and aligning with their gender psychology.
- Influence their mood instead of being influenced. When your spouse is in a bad mood, it's crucial not to follow them down the rabbit hole. Instead, adjust to where they are but don't let their mood control yours. Be supportive

and curious, giving them a space to vent and helping them relax. By being the one who sets a positive environment, you increase your Social Value and become someone they want to follow.
- In many struggling marriages, there is a trend of gender role reversal, where men feel weaker and women inadvertently present themselves as more masculine. To increase Social Value, it's important to align them with their gender psychology. Let men feel powerful and respected, and let women feel cherished and protected. By understanding and embracing these biological aspects, you can trigger a primal passion and desire in your spouse, creating a "*You're my prize*" mindset in their neurology. This alignment will contribute to increasing your Social Value and strengthening the relationship.

Weekly Wins
1. Great family vacation in Canada for my 50th. Lots of new experiences as individuals, and better to get to share it with each other. ▬▬ and the kids voluntarily expressed multiple times throughout the week what a great time we were all having together.
2. Great conversation with ▬▬ (in front of the kids)... ▬▬ asked if the reason I didn't do a particular thing was to avoid making her feeling frustrated; I answered "No, because I've learned that the approach of "happy wife, happy life...", then I paused in order to be very deliberate with my next words. ▬▬ completed my sentence, deliberately choosing her words and without any doubt in her mind, by saying "destroys marriages". It was affirmation that my living in touch with my MGR now is way more attractive to her and making our relationship more fulfilling to her.

Step 6 - Make them fall in love with you again

We've removed the Thorns that were keeping them away; And we've added so much Social Value that they're eager for your attention.

It is at this point that we can now make them fall in love with us again.

Think of it like when you first started dating.

You weren't in love with them straight away...

In fact, love was the last thing to happen.

You didn't have Thorns when you met, but you still had to, for instance, overcome your fear to talk to them.

Then, the first thing to develop is an attraction, an intrigue, a desire to spend time with them.

Only after do we develop love.

Here, it's the exact same thing.

A lot of people hear something like *"I'm not in love with you anymore!"* and (understandably) their world collapses...

They then either give up, because they have no idea how to make someone fall in love with them...

Or they aggressively try to force the spouse to fall in love with them, which does NOT work.

We have to walk them through the process of falling in love.

We can't just skip to the last step of the recipe and expect to have baked the cake.

A lot of people are even convinced it's "impossible" to make someone fall in love.

And if that's the strategy they're using, they're most certainly correct.

But we're smarter than that. We understand that there's a process by which people fall in love, and we're doing that with people every day.

And that's fulfilling their Prime Directives.

Unlike Love Languages, which is what you need for your spouse to know you love them. We're gonna show you how to fulfill Prime Directives.

Prime Directives are the boxes your spouse needs ticked in their brain in order to fall in love with you.

A lot of people think *"I just need to show my spouse I love them"*. That's not the problem anymore - we're past that. At this point they don't care if you love them, the problem is that they don't love you.

And that's fine, because we can change that with Prime Directives. We just need to identify and fulfill them.

This is also something no one else knows. So in breaking down your spouse's Prime Directives, you're also able to blow affair partners right out of the water.

Because whatever they can do, you'll be able to do far better. And you'll be able to tailor it to the emotional needs your spouse is most looking to fulfill.

Think of it this way - when they first fell in love with you, you didn't know about these metrics... so you, by happenstance, were able to get high scores, which translated into them falling in love.

If they have an affair, it means that after your scores dropped, the affair partner was able to score higher.

But when you know their Prime Directives, you know all the metrics they need, and you know how to score them. So the only thing stopping you from getting the maximum score is your decision to apply what you learned.

This is a 4 step process:

1. Identify their Prime Directive

PD's are responsible for how we think and feel, so they always manifest in how we act on a daily basis. If it makes it easier, you can think of it as "what kind of person we are". This is what you wrote down in Step 1;

2. Confirm their Control Drama

The lack of a PD creates an unmet need that will result in specific negative behaviors. These serve as your confirmation that you identified the correct PD;

3. Provide their Catalyst

Knowing what PD is lacking, we're now able to start providing them with what they need. This is what will allow us to fulfill them, and this is what makes them fall in love;

4. Speak in their Communication Style

Each PD has a different preferred communication style. If the Catalyst is what you need to give them, the Communication Style is how you need to deliver it. Using the wrong communication style is enough for them to reject your efforts.

So let's simplify with some examples...

In Step 1 I used a Power Prime Directive as an example.

So we identified they're "get shit done" kind of people. They're self-motivated, resilient, impatient, get frustrated easily when others struggle to follow directions, and love to be challenged.

Based on that, we can identify their Prime Directive is likely Power.

We can confirm this suspicion based on their recent behavior. If they got angry and got into an argument with you, resorting to ultimatums and sharp comments. This is their Control Drama, which we can use as confirmation of our diagnosis.

If their Control Drama is different, like giving you the cold shoulder and avoiding to even respond to you... we know we were probably wrong in our assessment and need to go back to the drawing board.

This step is important because we need to make sure that we have the right Prime Directive. So having this second layer to confirm our diagnosis is important and should never be skipped...

Assuming we'd gotten it right, we know that the Catalyst, the thing they need to fulfill their Prime Directive is faith in themselves and in their ability to overcome problems through sheer force of will...

What we need to build up in them is their own personal power... their belief in themselves, to break through obstacles and prove people wrong.

How we communicate that is also important. Because if we're submissive, they won't respect us. If we're lovey-dovey, doting on them, they won't feel any of it is genuine.

In fact, the tone you're going for is more like a rallying cry, or a motivational speech. That's what they'll respond to most.

Trying to have drawn out talks about emotions with these people will massively backfire...

But if you can make them believe they can conquer anything, they'll feel empowered to take on the world. And you'll cement your position as the person they always want by their side.

That is what gets Power people to fall in love.

> 🥰🥰 this past week there has been another shift with my husband, almost seemingly overnight. We had some moments of security conversations last week and I really was mindful of the gender role position, his power pd and really listening and accepting what he was sharing without interruption, or judgement, just compassion and agreement frame, instilling that faith catalyst in him (look at me now 😅). The next day and now 5 days in a row he's been contacting me frequently, calling me about everything civil, security, connection, he even planned a surprise visit with all the kids and also invited my parents for our sons birthday dinner. Then showed up again two days later for more family time. Was very affectionate and playful and just happy and relaxed. I do not have any expectations of when he'll ask me to come stay with him at our second home but I feel that he has turned a corner. I cannot be more hopeful right now and have so much gratitude and happiness for the positive movement forward for our family's future together. Today is awesome!

Using another example...

Let's say they're more on the sensitive side. They're big on communication, they're compassionate and caring, and big dreamers. This is indicative of a Love Prime Directive.

We can now confirm our suspicion if their recent behavior has been guilt tripping and gas lighting... playing the victim and rewriting history.

If we confirm we have the right Prime Directive, we now know what we need to do to get them to fall in love with you.

All you need to do is open up all the layers and connect with them at the most vulnerable level... and give them a glimpse of how much more there is to you than they thought.

You can't be direct with these people either... You have to ease slowly into it, to be very mindful of having a loving and nurturing tonality.

You need to talk about deep emotions, fears, shame, traumas, and insecurities, that you'd never shared so deeply before...

This is what Love people need from you to fall in love with you.

If we try and just guess, or try to cover our bases and do all of them, all we do is push them away. Because what works for one Prime Directive is detrimental to another.

But if you have clarity on their Prime Directive, reeling them in is so fun and easy that it becomes almost impossible for you to fail at this point.

And when they redevelop this strong, deep love for you... they also have a renewed and unshakable commitment to your relationship. Without you having to draw a 50 point presentation on why they should love you!

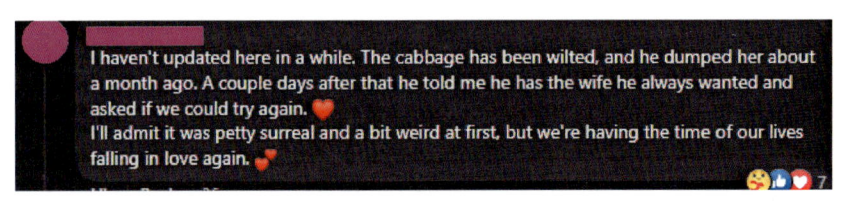

> I haven't updated here in a while. The cabbage has been wilted, and he dumped her about a month ago. A couple days after that he told me he has the wife he always wanted and asked if we could try again. ❤️
> I'll admit it was petty surreal and a bit weird at first, but we're having the time of our lives falling in love again. 💘

Cabbage = affair partner

Chapter takeaways:

- To make your spouse fall in love with you again, you need to identify and fulfill their Prime Directive. Prime Directives are the boxes your spouse needs ticked in their brain in order to fall in love with you. By understanding their Prime Directive and providing the Catalysts they need, you can create a strong foundation for love to develop.
- Always confirm their Control Drama. The lack of a Prime Directive creates unmet needs that manifest in specific negative behaviors, known as Control Dramas. By observing their recent behavior, you can confirm if your analysis of their Prime Directive is correct. If their Control Drama aligns with your assessment, it serves as

confirmation that you've identified the right Prime Directive.
- Each Prime Directive has a different preferred communication style. It's important to deliver your message in a way that resonates with their Communication Style. For example, if their Prime Directive is Power, a motivational and rallying communication style may be more effective. If their Prime Directive is Love, a nurturing and emotional communication style may be more impactful. Tailoring your communication style to their Prime Directive greatly increases the chances of them falling in love with you again.

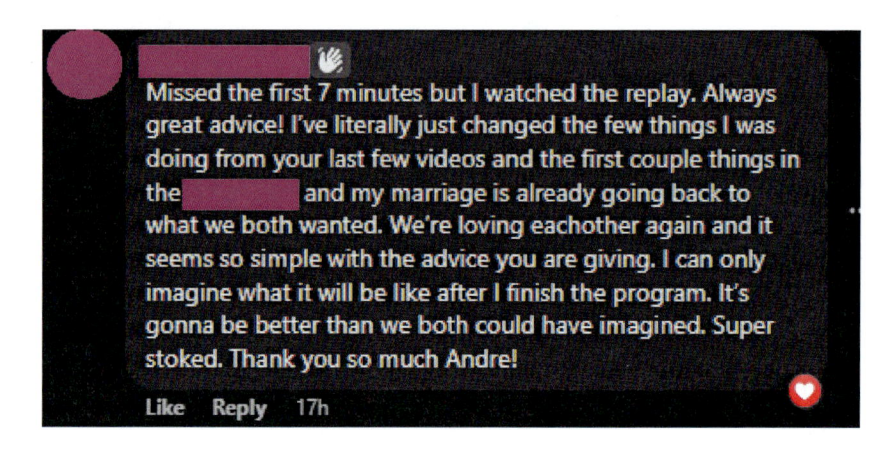

> 👋 Missed the first 7 minutes but I watched the replay. Always great advice! I've literally just changed the few things I was doing from your last few videos and the first couple things in the ▇▇▇ and my marriage is already going back to what we both wanted. We're loving eachother again and it seems so simple with the advice you are giving. I can only imagine what it will be like after I finish the program. It's gonna be better than we both could have imagined. Super stoked. Thank you so much Andre!
>
> Like   Reply   17h   ♥

Step 7 - Correct their behavior with Psychological Qualification

Einstein's definition of insanity is "doing the same thing over and over again, expecting a different result"...

If we don't change the destructive behavioral patterns for BOTH of you, then in time you'll end up in the same place.

Destructive behaviors will negatively affect you, them, and the relationship/family itself.

So it's not about changing quirks in them that you don't like. It's safeguarding the relationship from sabotage they don't have conscious control over...

Common examples of destructive behaviors that we may need to correct in our spouse can be:

Indecisiveness,
Control issues,
Jealousy,
Lying/omission,
Complaining,

Stubbornness,
Forgetfulness,
Etc...

You've done the Neural Makeover... so correcting your unhelpful behavior patterns is much easier.

They haven't, though...

So we need to be mindful of how we're doing this... because if we use the wrong approach, we're likely to generate resentment and Entrenchment against us...

Which is often the reason they asked for a divorce in the first place.

There are 3 Major Mistakes people make when they want to correct their spouse's behavior:

> **1. Attempting to correct their behavior too early will backfire.**

They need to recognize your high Social Value, and you need to fulfill their Prime Directives.

Otherwise, they have no reason to change their behavior. They need to want your approval, they need a carrot to chase.

If we're giving them feedback on what to change, but they feel they're settling for you... you'll just come across as more trouble than you're worth.

This will stack over time, and eventually they'll resent you.

2. Attempting to correct their behavior through Punishment will backfire.

Complaining, pointing out why they're wrong, making them feel guilty, making them feel dumb, or pointing out what they <u>shouldn't</u> do is going to instill negative feelings...

They'll start feeling dumb, guilty, they'll lose confidence in themselves, start questioning themselves, etc...

In the short term, it'll look like these strategies work... But after a certain amount of time, all they'll see is how you make them feel worse about themselves.

At that point, they'll start resenting you.

3. Attempting to correct their behavior directly into the final result will backfire.

If we take a black and white approach... in which our idea of what they should do is the only tolerable thing to do, and everything else is wrong... they'll feel they're being micromanaged, that your expectations are unrealistic, and they can't do anything right...

If we're not giving them wiggle room to grow and expand into more helpful behaviors, we'll stifle them... and after a while, they'll resent you for it.

So how do we change their negative behaviors without generating resentment?

That's where Psychological Qualification comes in.

Psychological Qualification means you're giving them positive traits they want to claim. And then using positive reinforcement to progressively guide them into those behaviors.

This means that instead of feeling bad about our feedback, they enjoy, appreciate it, and it's not uncommon that they start craving it...

Because instead of pointing out what they're doing wrong, we're using positive reinforcement to point out what they're doing right.

This builds the confidence they need to change their behavior...

And with Qualification we make them feel proud of their new wonderful qualities if they do the healthy behavior.

For instance:

If they're stubborn, instead of telling them they're stubborn and that they need to be more open to other people's ideas... which is what most people do... we'll get much farther with them if we instead pick a time they did hear you, and phrase it as:

"I really appreciate you hearing me out [specific situation when they did]. It's not easy to challenge our own thinking... so that really speaks a lot to your character, that you're devoted to truth, not ego, like most people seem to be..."

We're Qualifying them to be more open to listen to you. Because we're equating listening to having integrity, and not being driven by ego.

What do you think they'll want to do more of in the future? Be stubborn and egotistical? Or smarter and "better than most people"?

And instead of complaining that they're stubborn, or telling them they should be more open... we're rewarding them for the time they were open.

So we're not creating negative feelings of being scolded. We're creating positive feelings of being celebrated.

This isn't just the smartest and fastest way to change someone's behavior - it's also the kindest.

Keep reinforcing them in this way and you'll be surprised at how welcoming they become to your feedback. Because it makes them feel good - and they feel they're growing into a better version of themselves.

Remember that your spouse didn't go through this process. They didn't develop the self-awareness you did.

So their behaviors aren't because they intend to harm, they're a result of conditioned habits, fears and insecurities over which they have no awareness…

If we tell them their behaviors are wrong, they won't take it as "I'm doing something wrong", they'll take it as "I'm not good enough".

And that'll trigger Entrenchment and resentment.

But with Qualification, we help them heal and eliminate their insecurities. While at the same time changing their destructive behaviors.

Then you'll have a spouse who's receptive to hearing you out, who trusts you, wants to earn your time and attention, is madly in love with you, AND is willing to change for you too…

So you not only have the love of your life back - you keep them at your side.

To have and to hold, to love and cherish, until death do you part.

From ▇▇▇▇▇▇▇▇ to Everyone:
Yes it can happen! My husband isn't a person to really like or show affection. Now that things are so much better between us he has been more affectionate, holds my hand, etc

Chapter takeaways:

1. Avoid correcting their behavior too early, using punishment as a means of correction, or having unrealistic expectations. These approaches can backfire and generate resentment. Instead, focus on using Psychological Qualification to positively reinforce desired behaviors.
2. Psychological Qualification involves giving your spouse positive traits they want to claim and using positive reinforcement to guide them towards those behaviors. Instead of pointing out what they're doing wrong, focus on highlighting what they're doing right. This approach builds their confidence and makes them more receptive to change. This helps them heal their insecurities and conditioning, which can effectively change their destructive behaviors while fostering a stronger and more loving relationship.
3. Remember that your spouse may not have gone through the same process of self-awareness and growth as you have. Approach their behaviors with understanding and compassion, and use Psychological Qualification to guide them towards positive change.

Hi Awesome U Family,

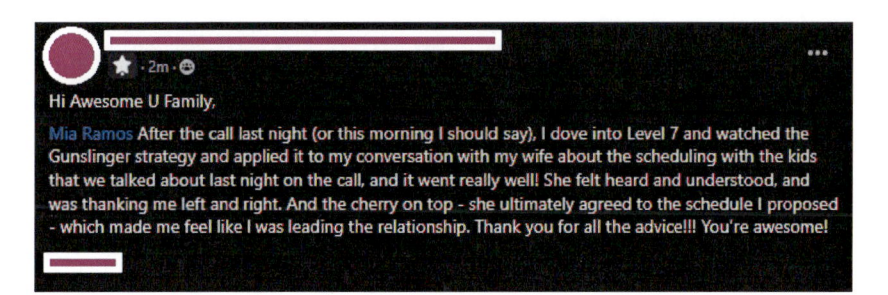

Mia Ramos After the call last night (or this morning I should say), I dove into Level 7 and watched the Gunslinger strategy and applied it to my conversation with my wife about the scheduling with the kids that we talked about last night on the call, and it went really well! She felt heard and understood, and was thanking me left and right. And the cherry on top - she ultimately agreed to the schedule I proposed - which made me feel like I was leading the relationship. Thank you for all the advice!!! You're awesome!

Success stories

You're probably wondering who this system has worked for, right?

Here are just a few of the success stories.

Case Study 1: Michelle (Operations Manager)

Before: Her husband was moving out of the house, their marriage was hanging by a thread and the more she tried to fix things, the more he pulled away. She didn't feel valued, seen, loved or a priority...

After: He's moved back in, and recommitted to her and their marriage. Their love and bond is stronger than she ever thought possible.

Story: Michelle is a high-achiever in everything she does, so feeling so powerless to change how her husband felt and acted was driving her into a depression fast. When she found out there was a system that allowed her to do that, she rolled up her sleeves, canceled her Netflix subscription, and started implementing the Science of Connection in every conversation with her husband.

She diligently implemented this system and now her husband - who was so dead set on divorce - is sending her flowers. And they listen to my videos together and share their insights with one another.

The best part? Because of how thorough she was in implementing the system, she achieved all of this in a mindblowing 3 weeks.

> **Michelle**
> My husband has been listening to replays of Andres live sessions with me. He thinks Andre is brilliant......duh..... We are communicating better than ever at a much deeper level. Whenever i say something profound in our discussions, he says "is that what Andre says?" lol..... enjoying life together. Word of advice, follow the steps and dont rush it. We had some significant life changing events despite me showing up as my better self. Training taught me how to handle it and that is why we are where we are today. (by my choice) Husband not living his own life anymore. He has stopped going to the bars and making excuses for his behavior. He is finally showing up as the husband i always wanted and needed. Trust the process and the outcome will be whatever YOU choose! You are in control! You are all so strong and amazing!

> My win for the week, my husband is back in more ways than one! Had a great V-day weekend away. So much fun, connection, and love! Me: " I love you" Him: "I love you more!" I believe it....thanks Andre and Mia and this totally awesome group! Have to keep the momentum going.

> We celebrated my birthday away as a family this past weekend but today was my birthday. He hasnt sent me flowers in years but it was such a nice suprise at work! It wasnt just the thought or the roses but what the note said! I feel blessed but couldnt have done it without this help and support! Thank you! XO " Love of a lifetime"

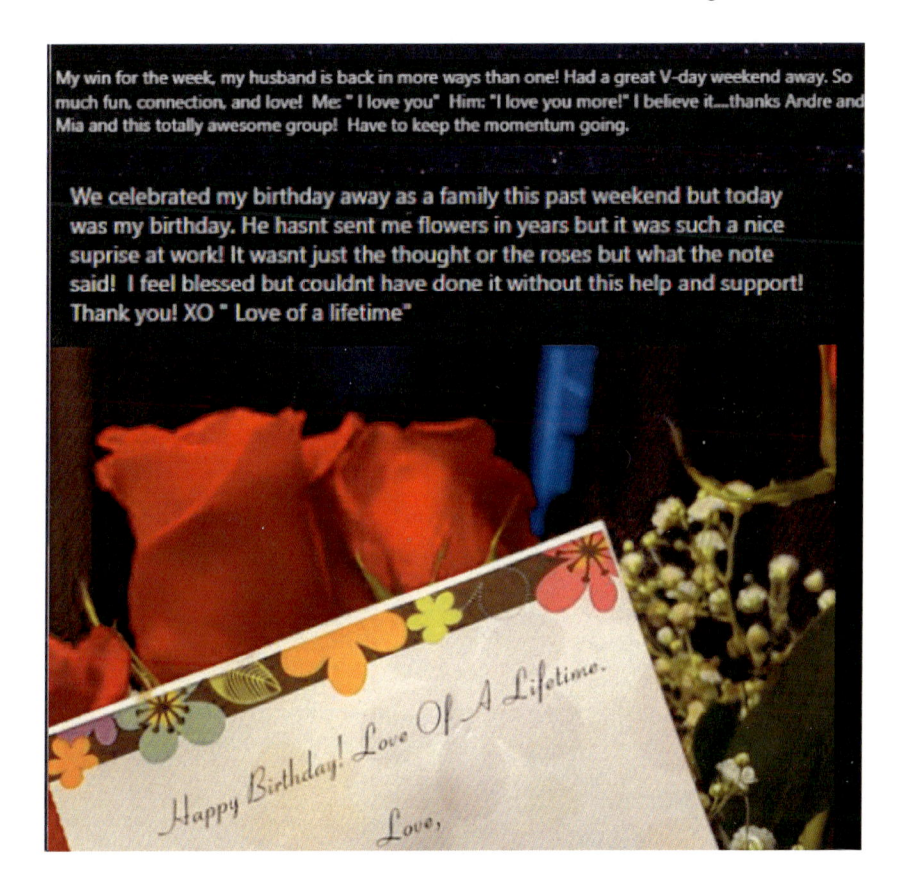

Case Study 2: Ben (Business Owner)

Before: Bent over backwards to please his wife and it was never good enough. Felt emasculated and was starting to doubt his worth as a man, and despite everything he did, she still wanted to leave him.

After: Now he's the man of the house, she's more attracted to him than she's ever been, and she's even using the tools in the Program for her own healing to please her husband.

Story: Ben is as busy as they come. He somehow juggles 3 jobs, and unsurprisingly, that took a massive toll on his marriage. Both in the time he had available for her, and in the stress he carried on his shoulders.

He arranged his schedule to have a single free afternoon, locked himself in his home office, and went through all of the Neural Makeover processes we have in our Coaching Program.

When he came back downstairs, he was a different man. And his wife noticed and commented immediately how "something is different about you".

He works the same hours, but stress is a thing of the past, and whatever time they do have together is high-quality time. She's head-over-heels with her husband again, she started studying the Program on her as well… And they routinely talk about their take-aways with each other over morning coffee.

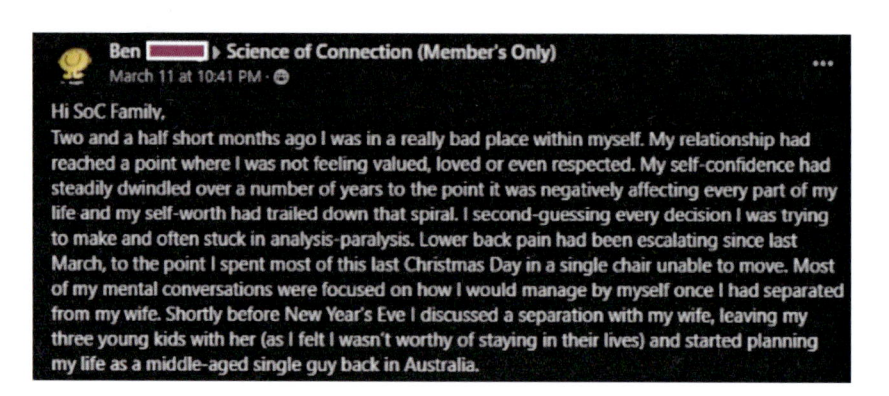

> **Ben ▬▬▬ ▸ Science of Connection (Member's Only)**
> March 11 at 10:41 PM ·
>
> Hi SoC Family,
> Two and a half short months ago I was in a really bad place within myself. My relationship had reached a point where I was not feeling valued, loved or even respected. My self-confidence had steadily dwindled over a number of years to the point it was negatively affecting every part of my life and my self-worth had trailed down that spiral. I second-guessing every decision I was trying to make and often stuck in analysis-paralysis. Lower back pain had been escalating since last March, to the point I spent most of this last Christmas Day in a single chair unable to move. Most of my mental conversations were focused on how I would manage by myself once I had separated from my wife. Shortly before New Year's Eve I discussed a separation with my wife, leaving my three young kids with her (as I felt I wasn't worthy of staying in their lives) and started planning my life as a middle-aged single guy back in Australia.

> Fast-forward to now and I'm in Week 10 of the coaching program, and I find myself living a life that I never even knew was possible for me. Here are a few highlights:
>
> *My wife and I are not only still together, but stronger than ever before, including our emotional and physical connection.
>
> *Living in my male gender role is having me show up in ways that she's never seen me before, and she's regularly telling me the positive difference it's having on her.
>
> *I have more confidence in every area of my life than I can ever recall having. This is showing up in the relationship, at work and even as a parent. An unexpected bonus is the positive ripple effect my new way of being is having on my kids.
>
> *I've been able to drop the heavy chains of gestalts and limiting beliefs that held me back for as long as I can remember, and I've left the 'people-pleaser' identity way behind me now.
>
> *My wife asked me after week 3 of the coaching program if she could start doing some of the exercises, based on the changes she was seeing in me. She's now caught up to me in the course content and we debrief our most recent breakthroughs over our morning coffee date, which has now become the part of our day we both look forward to most.
>
> *We're discussing things we didn't previously talk about at super-deep levels, such as what we *really* want out of life on a daily, weekly, monthly and long-term basis, and how we can best support each other to have and be all of those things. We've found alignment on parenting challenges where previously we weren't, including conversations that have helped us understand why we've had conflicting views on some areas in the past.
>
> *I've lost 13 pounds, become much fitter and now have zero back pain.
>
> The future now fills me with excitement and a sense of gratitude for all that is now in my life.
>
> I have no doubt that I would be in a very different place, on all levels, if I had not found SoC exactly when I did.
>
> Andre – thank you for making this all possible, and all of the SoC crew - coaches and community – for adding all that you do to this incredible program.
>
> And to any of you that read this post, I hope that something in my story thus far helps you in some way, whatever way you may be looking for!
>
> 💜

Case Study 3: Rebecca (Pharmacy Supervisor)

Before: Husband was in a 2 year-long affair/serious relationship with another woman, and wanted to leave Rebecca to start a family with her.

After: Now, he has left the affair, blocked her on all social media, and is head-over-heels in love with Rebecca again.

Story: Rebecca came in with the right mindset. She was humble, receptive, ready to learn, and welcomed being pushed out of her comfort zone.

She was exhausted because every interaction turned into a heated argument, and she was ready for change.

So when she told me about her husband's affair, I outlined a plan with her to flip switches in his brain about the affair partner. She did. And the very next time I spoke to her, she told me how her husband had just broken up the affair because of the steps she'd taken.

After that, during a boat party, he was literally holding and cuddling with Rebecca to ward off the women that wanted to flirt with him.

It took her two months to go from constant arguments and a serious affair, to a loving and romantic relationship with her husband again.

And now that she's conquered Social Value and his Prime Directives, her biggest relief is that she doesn't have to worry about him cheating ever again.

> From Rebecca ▆▆ to Me: (Privately)   10:26 PM
> so if I can't end up staying, I had one HUGE win this week. The mistress is gone!!! there has been no communication, texts, Facebook likes, etc since before my birthday!!! I found out this week and I was just floored!!! I never thought it would happen!!!

> **Rebecca** ▆▆
> I can't believe how far we've come in such a short amount of time. When I started I wasn't sure if our marriage could be saved and I was positive divorce papers would be given to me any day and honestly, I had been looking into divorce myself because I couldn't see things getting any better. I'm so thankful that I found you Mia and Andre and this program! You have helped me turn everything around!

> **Rebecca** ▨
>
> Huge win today!! I just got surprised at work with flowers from ▨!! He never sends flowers!!! And there was a beautiful note tucked in them as well. Thank you Andre for your help and guidance!!! If I hadn't found you, I'm pretty sure I'd be divorced right now!!!

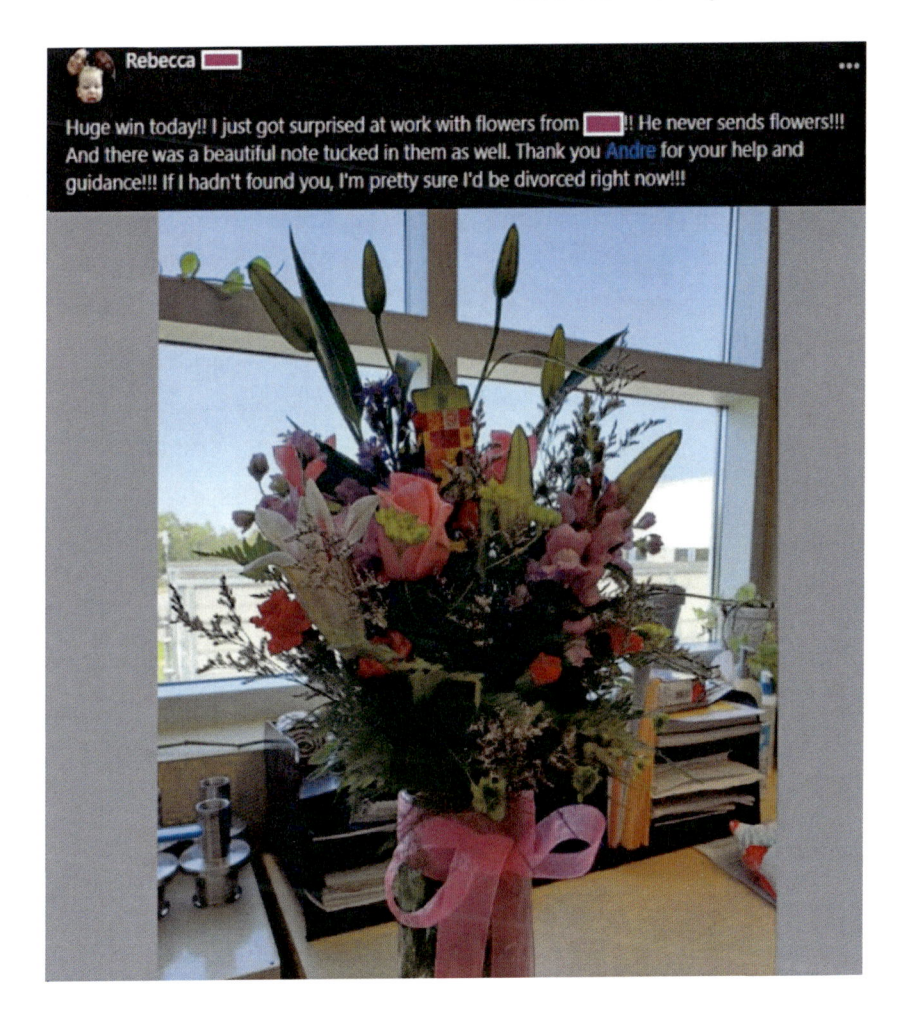

Case Study 4: Ellen (Therapist)

Before: Her "impossibly closed off" husband moved into the basement while going through the divorce proceedings. She felt powerless because he was super stoic and impossible to get him to open up about emotion.

After: She got him to come back to the bedroom, scrap the divorce talk, hold her hand and show affection, and even talking about his feelings with her.

Story: Right from the moment she joined, Ellen was as humble and diligent as they come. She'd message us after our Coaching Calls to express her heartfelt gratitude for the effort, energy, and sacrifice we were investing in our clients, and that just made coaching her a breeze.

Her husband was a very logical person, used to being in charge, and it was "impossible to change his mind". But that didn't stop her from wanting to learn how to change his heart.

Initially, he was adamant in kicking her out and sending her to live 8 hours away without her kids.

But after only 3 weeks of joining our Coaching Program, she was getting hugs and cuddles from this stoic man.

A few months later, their relationship had only improved, and she updated us to let us know her husband was like a changed man - caring and romantic.

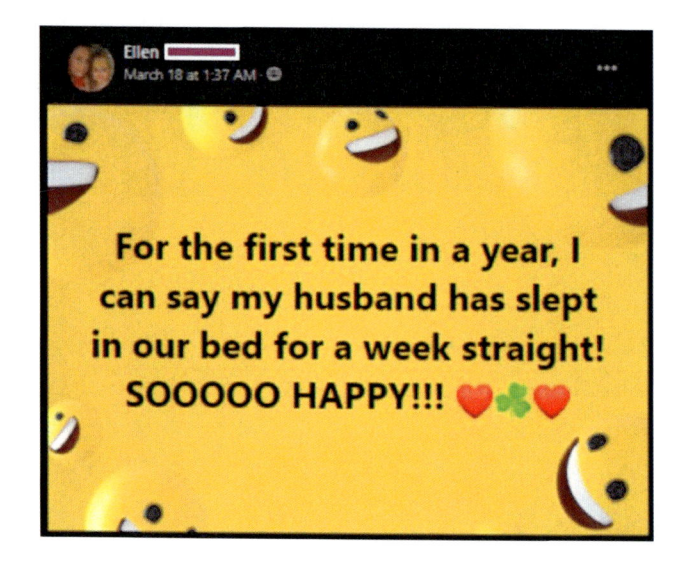

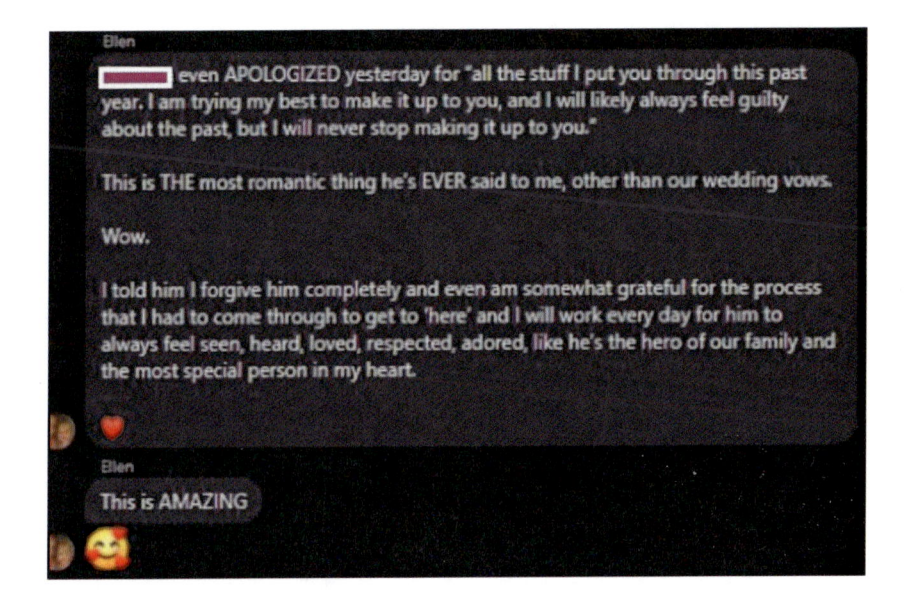

> Ellen
>
> ▬▬▬ even APOLOGIZED yesterday for "all the stuff I put you through this past year. I am trying my best to make it up to you, and I will likely always feel guilty about the past, but I will never stop making it up to you."
>
> This is THE most romantic thing he's EVER said to me, other than our wedding vows.
>
> Wow.
>
> I told him I forgive him completely and even am somewhat grateful for the process that I had to come through to get to 'here' and I will work every day for him to always feel seen, heard, loved, respected, adored, like he's the hero of our family and the most special person in my heart.
>
> ♥
>
> Ellen
> This is AMAZING
> 😊

Case Study 5: Jason (Marine)

Before: His wife called him abusive because of his military style of communication, she moved out and asked for a divorce.

After: Within two weeks of using our communication formulas, she moved back in and apologized for not being more understanding.

Story: Jason didn't think he would ever be able to communicate with his wife because of how conditioned he'd been from his military career.

His wife was dead set on divorce, and even though he didn't believe it was even possible to change her mind, he refused to give up without at least putting in his 100%.

Over the first two weeks working together, he was a new man, and I taught him how to disentrench her and Pluck her Thorns. So that weekend when she came round the house to pick up the last of her stuff, he applied those strategies, disentrenched her, and they had a deep and meaningful conversation.

He did such a great job on that one conversation that she moved back home soon after because of it. And a few weeks later, she joined him in going through the Program too.

> To update you guys she just left. We sat the dining Room table for about 45 minutes and just had a long heart to heart talk. 😊 I tell you all just looking into her eyes again makes me melt. 😊 Andre Santos i followed your advice about what to say when she started going to the divorce topic. She stopped talking and was intensely listening to me, and for the first time in a long time when I said I may move on and I won't ever look back once I close this door. I saw a tear come down her cheek. She brought up how lonely she was and she missed our long conversations we used to have. 😊 Then she started talking about how much she missed our intimacy prior to 6 months ago. I was sitting there trying to not smile or start jumping up and down, because that is exactly how I am feeling. 😊😊 She really opened up to me and I was not pushing or even touching her because I wanted her to feel safe. At one point as we were leaving she put her hand on my shoulder, and I never realized how good it felt to be touched by her. 😊😊😊😊 We went to Costco I bought her some

> towels and some Tupperware that she wanted. I really felt like she enjoyed our time together like I did. We stood in the parking lot talking for about another 30 minutes. She invited me to go tonight to a kids dance recital a friend of ours; their kid is in. And then she grabbed me and gave me a deep sincere hug. 😊😊😊😊 I stood there for about 2 seconds with my hands to my side before my brain was like dude hug her back!! I was in shock. I never thought she would hug me again like that. 😌 I almost cried I was so happy feeling her love. I pick her up at 5 tonight for the recital. I know I still have a lot of personal stuff I need to work on and I definitely need to continue working on my communication continually. I can't wait to see what the future Has in store for me. If it wasn't for you guys and Andre's advice I know I wouldn't be here now. She even said she noticed I'm not the same person she left. 😊😊😊 I can't wait to get to next week with you guys. I'm 100% a believer in Andre Mia and everyone in here!!!! Today was a success because of you guys and the hours and hours of video and posts on here I've been reading and watching!! Love you guys. You are making a difference in my life so sincerely thank you!!!! 😊😊😊

Case Study 6: Lacie (Nurse)

Before: Her husband started an affair that developed into a serious relationship, and he even left her to move in with the affair partner.

After: She not only got him back home, she got him to cut off all contact with the ex-affair partner and become the romantic husband she fantasized with.

Story: Lacie's husband had moved in with the affair partner, and had become a parent to her kids too, so he told Lacie he'd never leave the other woman because he had to think of her kids. This shattered Lacie, especially since he seemed to have had no problem walking out on their 5 kids together… But she refused to let that defeat her.

Instead, she buckled up, studied the system, applied it, asked for feedback, corrected what needed correcting, rinse and repeat.

As she filled his Prime Directives, suddenly his mind changed... He broke things off with the other woman, moved back in with Lacie, and became the husband and father Lacie always believed he could be.

He's also more romantic now than he'd ever been, and Lacie feels she's back in her honeymoon with him.

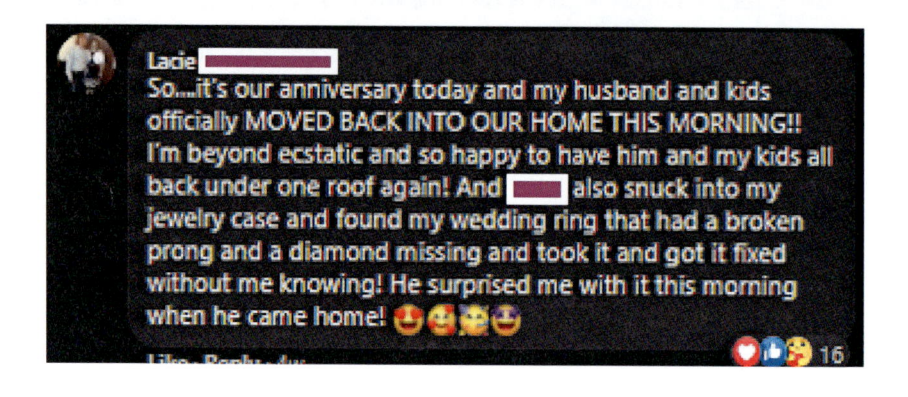

> He made me a card for my birthday. I wanted to share what he wrote. This is from the guy who, just 6 weeks ago, couldn't stand to be in the same room with me and wanted to file for divorce ASAP. 😅
>
> Oh, a couple years ago his wedding ring was damaged and we never bothered to replace it. He hasn't worn one since. Imagine my surprise when, this morning, out of the blue, he sent me links to wedding rings he likes. He said he wanted to get a new one very soon because he missed wearing one.
>
> I'll admit it's a bit awkward as we try and navigate our new dynamic, and figure out what we're doing. It's a lot like building a new relationship. But it's getting easier, and we're having so much fun falling in love with each other again. ❤️

> **Lacie** ▬▬▬▬▬
> So....it's our anniversary today and my husband and kids officially MOVED BACK INTO OUR HOME THIS MORNING!! I'm beyond ecstatic and so happy to have him and my kids all back under one roof again! And ▬▬▬ also snuck into my jewelry case and found my wedding ring that had a broken prong and a diamond missing and took it and got it fixed without me knowing! He surprised me with it this morning when he came home! 😃😅🥰😄
>
> ❤️👍😲 16

> They are home!!!! I'm so beyond excited 🤗
>
> And ▓▓▓▓ must have snuck into my jewelry and took my wedding ring and got it fixed because he gave it to me this morning when he came home. 😅😄 he is amazing and I feel so loved!

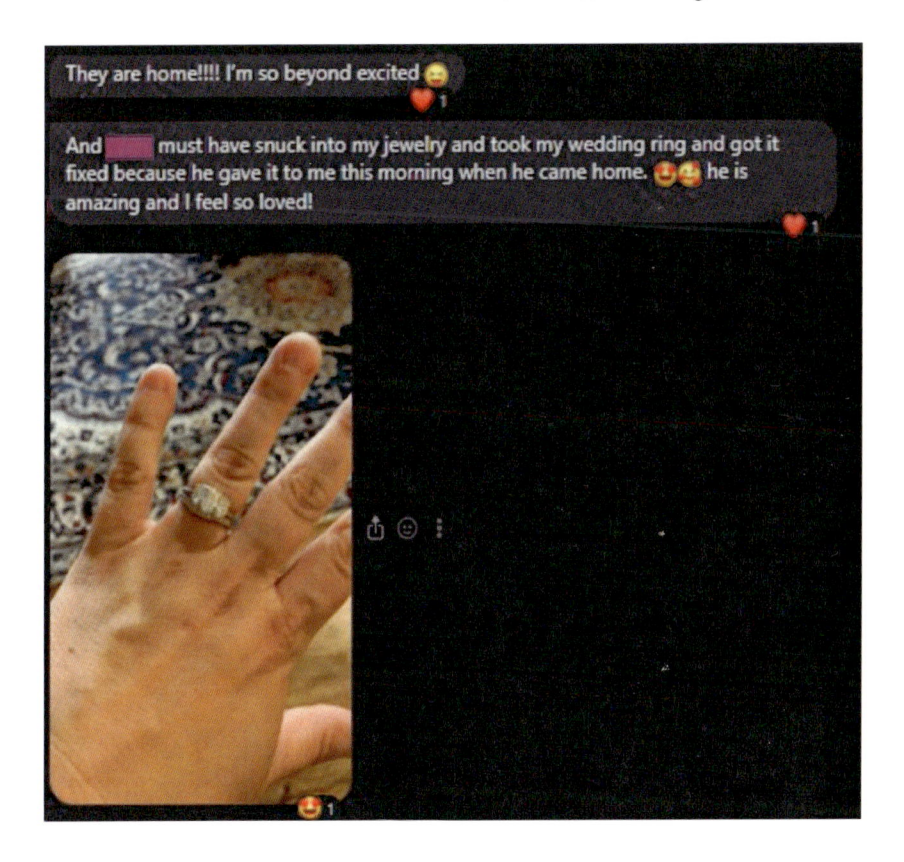

What To Do Next

The Science of Connection can help you save your marriage and transform how your spouse feels about you. Even if they're completely convinced there's no hope and aren't willing to put any effort in.

So to recap, to become a Relationship Jedi - able to break through your spouse's defenses, stop the divorce talks, and get them to fall back in love with you - you need to:

- Identify the levers in their brain that are keeping them stuck, and the criteria they need to fall in love.
- Go through your Neural Makeover to become the very best version of you as fast as possible.
- Dig them out of their Entrenchment with the levers you uncovered earlier - so they trust and are open to communicating with you.
- Pluck the Thorns that are at the root of the problems in your relationship.
- Build your Social Value so they're the ones chasing you.

- Fulfill their Prime Directives so they can't help but to fall in love with you.
- Change any destructive behaviors that could spell trouble later - with Qualification and positive reinforcement.

You can do it alone, which is extremely challenging. It took me 7 years to figure this out and refine it.

Or you can take the easy path and work with me.

If you work with me, my team and I will do this process with you. You'll get results much faster than if you were to do it alone, and you'll have the certainty you're doing every step right.

You'll have expert eyes and advanced tools to decode the Matrix and identify the levers we need to change how your spouse feels about you (Prime Directives, Thorns, Trust Types, Beliefs, and Fears)...

You'll be able to finish your Neural Makeover before the end of the week, instead of spending a year in therapy "working on yourself"...

You'll be able to Disentrench your spouse no matter what they say (we'll craft your texts with you to cover all possible scenarios)...

You can forget about paying lawyers, battling for custody, and losing your assets. Because you'll have proven formulas to Pluck Thorns so you can stop the divorce in its tracks...

You'll be able to get your spouse wrapped around your finger (we'll rebalance your Gender Roles and build massive stacks of Social Value)...

You can forget about their affair, because we'll turn the levers in your spouse's brain to get them to break things off with the affair partner too (and turn to you with undying loyalty)...

You'll be able to fulfill their Prime Directives effortlessly and have them worship the ground you walk on (we'll even decode their Prime Directives for you)...

You'll be able to correct their destructive behaviors so you can build your happily-ever-after. And have them drop to their knees to thank you for not having given up on them.

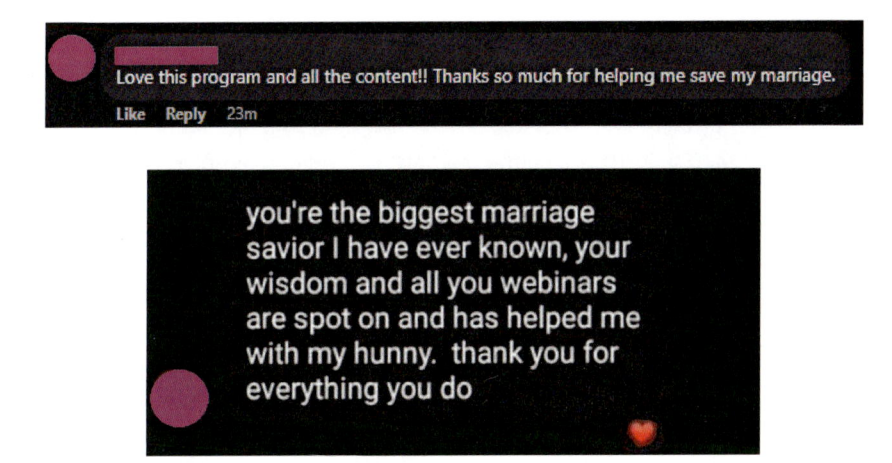

> Love this program and all the content!! Thanks so much for helping me save my marriage.
> Like   Reply   23m

> you're the biggest marriage savior I have ever known, your wisdom and all you webinars are spot on and has helped me with my hunny. thank you for everything you do ♥

This is NOT therapy.

This is a step-by-step gameplan where my team and I work directly with you and will be holding your hand to implement the entire process.

It is expensive, but you get what you pay for and unlike anyone else in this space, I guarantee results.

Our clients have gone from the brink of divorce to back in a committed relationship again in 90 days or less.

We've got limited spots, so if you'd like our help with this, book a call below and we'll walk you through the details.

Book a call in ***www.science-of-connection.com***

Again, this is for determined individuals who want to put an end to the divorce talks for good and save their marriage in 90 days, even if your spouse isn't on board...

Speak soon.

> Seriously this was the program that made everything start falling into place. I was completely without hope but also determined if this didn't work in 6-weeks I was DONE. Well Andre and the team delivered! We were communicating and even going on dates by the end (actually sooner) of the 6-weeks. Now about 4-months since completing the 6-week challenge, no more cabbage, long conversation, improved communication, all over the map of interaction (that will make sense once in the program), overall confidence in myself and our relationship.
>
> Love   Reply   2d   ❤️👍😊 7

> Best investment I have EVER made, life changing for me, my marriage, and our future generations.
>
> Like   Reply   18m

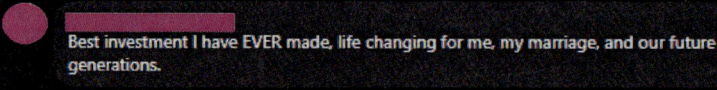

Q&A

Q: *"Does this work with stubborn and emotionally unavailable spouses?"*

Yes. Those are two problems that conventional therapy can't help, but our system is designed to work even better with these people.

Q: *"Will this work if my spouse is in a relationship with someone else?"*

Yes. We've worked with hundreds of people in this situation. There are levers in their brain that the affair partner was able to turn. We can turn them back, so they fall out of love with the affair partner, and we can have you turn all the right levers for them to fall in love with you instead.

Some of their spouses had 2 year long affairs and even proposed to the affair partner.

But that didn't matter once we turned the right levers.

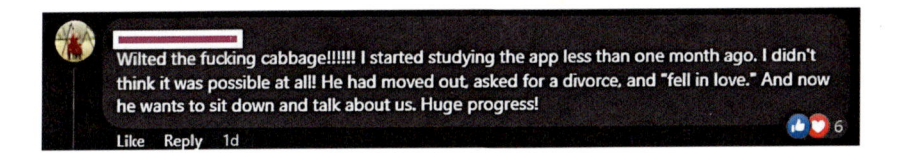

> Wilted the fucking cabbage!!!!!! I started studying the app less than one month ago. I didn't think it was possible at all! He had moved out, asked for a divorce, and "fell in love." And now he wants to sit down and talk about us. Huge progress!
> Like   Reply   1d   6

Q: *"Is this in a group setting?"*

Yes. Having a small and supportive group of people going through this at the same time keeps you accountable. It also helps you learn faster by practicing with the group before applying the techniques with your partner.

Q: *"Does this work with spouses going through a midlife crisis?"*

Absolutely. A midlife crisis is the result of feeling powerless over a long period of time. This is then manifested as a rebellion, which makes it feel like it came out of the blue.

We've helped so many people reeling their spouses back from a midlife crisis. And every single time the root cause of it was either an unfulfilled Prime Directive, Gender Role Reversal, or a drop in Social Value. If either of these aren't corrected for a long enough period of time, they'll trigger a midlife crisis.

We can help you to help them overcome that.

Q: *"What if I'm not able to speak to my spouse?"*

So long as you're legally able to contact them, we can get them to stop ghosting you and change how they feel.

Q: *"Do I need my spouse to do this with me?"*

Not at all. Almost all of our clients did this process without their spouse.
Our entire method is designed around changing how your spouse feels about you, without them having to be on board. If they are, great. If not, we never needed them to, in the first place. 😉

Q: *"My divorce is finalizing in less than 90 days. Can I speed up the process?"*

Absolutely. You only need to Disentrench them and Pluck the Thorns for them to no longer want the divorce. We've had people doing that as quickly as just two weeks. The rest of the time is to rebuild your dream relationship.

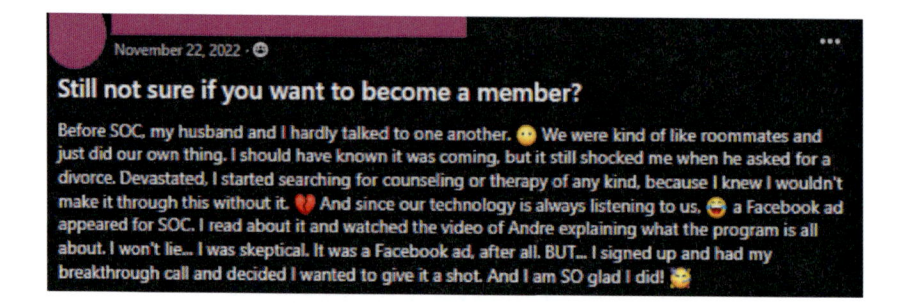

November 22, 2022

Still not sure if you want to become a member?

Before SOC, my husband and I hardly talked to one another. 😳 We were kind of like roommates and just did our own thing. I should have known it was coming, but it still shocked me when he asked for a divorce. Devastated, I started searching for counseling or therapy of any kind, because I knew I wouldn't make it through this without it. 💔 And since our technology is always listening to us, 😅 a Facebook ad appeared for SOC. I read about it and watched the video of Andre explaining what the program is all about. I won't lie... I was skeptical. It was a Facebook ad, after all. BUT... I signed up and had my breakthrough call and decided I wanted to give it a shot. And I am SO glad I did! 🤗

The amount of internal healing I've done through this program has been incredible. 💪 More than I even knew I could. I couldn't be more grateful for the tools I've learned for better communication and just life in general. Not to mention the most amazing coaches you'll ever meet! Being able to really talk to my husband without either one of us getting upset or frustrated is something I never thought possible! 🤯

One of my friends told me just the other day that something had been bothering her and she decided to talk to her husband about it in a calm, mature way. She said that was all thanks to me! 🤗 My husband and I get along better now than ever before. I don't know where I would be without this program. 💜 It was the best decision I have ever made!

About the Author

Andre is an expert and savant in human psychology. His background for decades was studying Psychology and combining it with Engineering principles to predict human behavior. Then using that to deescalate conflict and persuade leaders to make big decisions.

He pioneered this hybrid form of Psychology and Engineering because he was dissatisfied with the conventional models of Psychology. And he's responsible for numerous breakthroughs in that field now that allowed him to map out the factors at play in human decision making.

Now he's helping clients use these strategies in their marriages, and the results have been amazing.

Andre's worked with hundreds of individuals who didn't have their spouse's support in saving their marriage. And he took them from the brink of divorce to a loving and committed relationship again.

Andre's unique approach to communication and relationships relies on understanding the absolute truths about the spouse's brain, and their unique subjective realities, providing an effective and reliable method to reconnect with them.

As the creator of Science of Connection, and the CEO of Awesome U, Andre has worked tirelessly to implement this system with his clients. His unmatched success rate reflects his dedication to this system, and to his every client.

Aside from his professional life, Andre enjoys spending quality time with his wife, walking his puppy, practicing martial arts, he's a fan of all things nerdy, and has fun complaining about how scientifically inaccurate the movie is during date night.

In this book, he shares secret knowledge that he hopes will help men and women alike tap into the Relationship Jedi within, and transform their marriages. All without needing the spouse to be on board to begin with.

Here's How To Use The Science Of Connection To Save Your Marriage

Many people are able to figure things out with the spouse if they're both actively working on it. The problem is if your spouse has already given up, refuses to even try, and actively tells you there's no chance of getting them back.

That's where I come in. I help aspiring Relationship Jedi just like you to break through to their spouses and flip the switches in their brain that change how they feel about you and your marriage.

> **Step 1:** We decode their Matrix so we have a list of all the switches we need to flip.
> **Step 2:** We use special communication formulas to rebuild trust & resolve the issues between you at lightspeed.
> **Step 3:** We flip the switches that get them to fall in love and bend over backwards for you.

Most people are stuck in their old ways, thinking it's impossible to change someone's mind if they're not willing to change.

I've proven otherwise.

Now with my help, you can make this your reality too.

If you'd like to get started, hit this link to Book a Call with my team at *www.science-of-connection.com* and we'll take it from there.

Made in United States
North Haven, CT
24 January 2025